THE ART
of
ANTON MOSIMANN

THE ART
of
ANTON MOSIMANN

ANTON MOSIMANN

Photographs by Tom Belshaw

DEDICATION

To Philipp and Mark

A really good cuisine demands a single-minded,
almost holy, devotion. Success depends on
perfection in the smallest details.

Contents

Above Admiring the Cellnet racing car with Peter Waller from Cellnet. I have always had a fascination for cars and a passion for driving. *Right* Relaxing and enjoying the ambience of my dining club.

*I*t gives me great pleasure to welcome you to *The Art of Anton Mosimann*. This venture is very precious to me, allowing, as it does, the chance to reflect on the way in which my work has evolved so far.

For years I have pursued my craft, always striving to attain perfection in quality, taste, colour, texture and form – all equally important.

I create, and for a time I am satisfied, then I am inspired to create anew . . . this is my art.
I was eager that this book should be of the highest calibre to represent the standards implicit in my philosophy. It would not have been possible to produce such a work without the support of my friends at Cellnet.

They understand my quest for quality, for we are both committed to excellence at all times in our respective fields – I in my craft, Cellnet in offering the best service in cellular communications.

Cellnet and I also share an interest in motor racing; it is one of my favourite ways of relaxing. Encouraged by mutual interests and the pursuit of excellence we have developed this project together.

By giving their financial support, Cellnet have enabled me to create a book of superior quality and to make it available to the public at a realistic price. For this I thank them; long may they continue to support the finer things in life.

MY PHILOSOPHY AND MY FOOD

Right I have a special affection for fish – its freshness, the many varieties and colours, and the constant challenge of cooking it creatively. Cooking fish demands feeling and care, and it is a continual joy.

My style of cooking has always been to use the most perfect ingredients and to prepare them in the way best suited to them – simply – so as to bring out their colour, flavour, succulence and natural goodness. In many respects, my philosophy of food and life are the same: both should be an experience of happiness, serenity and joyful giving. These principles have developed from a broad range of experiences within my profession as well as from contact with people of many cultures and differing lifestyles. To explain how these opinions have evolved, I should like to share some memories with you.

Always a Chef

I was born with a wooden spoon in my mouth. My parents owned a farm and a small family restaurant near Solothurn in Switzerland and there they combined a practical knowledge of the demands of rearing and growing food with the simple, essential, skills of its preparation. I spent the first five years of my life in this homely environment of hard work. I have always loved the look and feel of fine ingredients, and I am sure that my early introduction to the most complete meaning of food served to instil this appreciation deeply. The gracious old city of Solothurn, with its cobbled streets, sparkling fountains and chiming bell towers, was the background to those early childhood years.

An only child, I grew up to be closely protected, but in an adult environment of hard work. There were no other children at home, so my parents' friends were my friends too. At school I always seemed older than the other boys in my class. When I was very young – just five years old – we moved to a restaurant in Nidau, and it was there that I decided that I wanted to be a chef. Within the confines of that pine-panelled, cosy restaurant I learned about cooking, about how to please

At five years old with a dear, childhood friend who used to escort me to school each day, five miles on foot in both directions.

people, and about working towards achieving an aim. I walked to and from school, five miles each way, on freezing, dark winter nights as well as during the hotter days of summer. At the end of the day, the warm glow of the beamed restaurant always welcomed me and I would sit on the carved chairs to do my homework. My school teacher, Erwin Allemanne, encouraged me to concentrate on my school work, scolding and praising as was necessary. I loved to cook even then – cheese fondue and spaghetti bolognese are the first dishes that I remember cooking at about the age of six. I also amused myself preparing meals for friends from the village, for adult friends who I came in contact with everyday as well as for my school pals.

One day, when I was twelve, I saw a beautiful new car on the street – a Chevrolet Corvair. I was transfixed. I walked around it, admiring it and dreamed of owning a similar car. I was determined that one day I should make enough money to do so. I went home, sat down and plotted ways of earning enough money to pass my driving test and buy a car by the time I was eighteen. I was single-minded and I put my plans into action: I sold old newspapers; I bred rabbits, and sold them to butchers; I even started to buy and sell old bicycles and radios. In fact I worked at anything to make money. Soon I was employing school friends, paying them pocket money for their help and working even harder myself. At eighteen I passed my driving test and, with Mother's help for the last of the essential cash, I bought a new Triumph Spitfire.

By the time I was fourteen I was also successful at sport, especially running and wrestling. Some teachers advised me to become a professional sportsman but I knew that I should enjoy life as a chef and nobody could change my mind.

At nineteen I saw an advertisement for a farmhouse which was for sale and I decided to sell the car and to invest all my savings in the property. As I was still too young to sign all the legal documents, the owner of the property indulged me and waited for a whole year until I was able to enter the contract and purchase the property at twenty. It turned out to be an astute business move.

My childhood and youth was a full and happy one during which I learnt to prize a simple balance in life – to appreciate the good things that came my way but not to forget or look down on those who were less fortunate. The people of Switzerland are renowned for their hospitality, which is in so great a contrast to the often harsh climate. My parents taught me that you can bring happiness to people in simple, generous ways. At Christmas they would open the restaurant and invite anyone who was alone to come in to share the festivities without charge.

A Strict Apprenticeship

Any good cook is an eternal apprentice. For me this role began at fifteen when I was invited to embark on my first course of training at the Hotel Baeren in Twann. There I learnt how to work. It was, I am still certain, one of the hardest apprenticeships imaginable, quite divorced from the approach of modern management and without any concern for motivation. I worked six days a week, scrubbing floors, cleaning copper pans and doing any general kitchen work, from eight in the morning and rarely did I finish before eleven at night. Every afternoon I spent my free hour writing up notes and preparing for the time that I spent away from the kitchens when I worked for five hours at college, learning to cook. The train into town, and the college, left fifteen minutes after I finished work in the kitchens but I was never allowed to leave early. I had to rush from the kitchen to

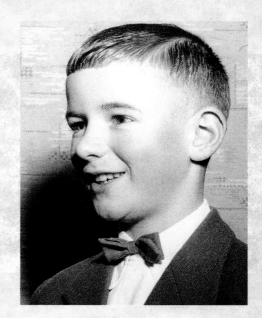

Aged ten, and in a bow-tie already. My mother insisted that I should be well-dressed from the earliest age.

my room to change, then run to the station to catch the train at the very last second. When I eventually crawled into bed, exhausted, I sometimes cried myself to sleep.

Despite my desperate tiredness I did everything I could to achieve a high standard. For example, it was standard practice to give the staff packet or canned soup for their meals and I was told to heat it up; instead I would get up extra early to prepare vegetables and make the soup properly.

For thirty-five years the tradition at the Hotel Baeren was to send young chefs who had completed their apprenticeships on to a hotel in Arosa. Reports from others who had followed this course of training led me to feel that the hotel in Arosa was not for me. Without the chef's knowledge, I applied to the Palace Hotel at Villars for the post of *commis de cuisine* following my apprenticeship.

The day came when I had to go to Berne to take the exams for the *Diplôme de Cuisinier*. I was seventeen and younger than the three other local candidates. It was a very difficult day, particularly for me, an outsider who had never worked in the kitchens before. I still remember the day vividly: the butchery test was followed by filleting fish and jointing a chicken, before going on to cook a three-course meal. We all worked individually, at our own stoves, without any help. In the afternoon we had to cost out the meal which we had prepared. At seven o'clock in the evening we were sitting in a small room, awaiting the results. The door opened and I was called in front of the examiners to be congratulated on passing. The others had all failed for one reason or another, and I was left quite speechless. I was happy for myself, yet sad for the others who had to wait another year before they could re-take the exams.

Above Aged seventeen, this photograph was taken at the ceremony at which I received the *Diplôme de Cuisinier*.

I went back to tell my chef with mixed feelings. He was happy at my success and announced that I could move on to Arosa. My confession of the secret application brought forth shocked and annoyed exclamations. This was the first time that anyone had questioned his judgement and he could not understand how I should know anything about quality or how I could know what I wanted to achieve. After a long discussion the chef accepted my decision and appreciated why I had taken such a step. It was the best decision I ever made.

My First Job

In 1964 I went to work at the Palace Hotel at Villars, under the strict regime of Henri Dessibourg, and that was when I began to understand the meaning of perfection. Nobody could have given me more than Monsieur Dessibourg who resembled the archetypal chef. At the age of fifty-five, his tummy rounded, he wore a tall hat and spoke only in French; he was a demanding character. Everything had to be perfect. No vegetable was allowed to pass unless it was of equal quality and size to its neighbour; not one item of food was allowed to leave the kitchen unless it was perfect. Once we had to cook two hundred and twenty Wiener Schnitzel and they all had to be identical in colour and doneness. There were forty of us cooks in the kitchen with a German chef as second in command. He shouted even louder and threw things even further than Monsieur Dessibourg. Looking back, I realise that it was good training and I am proud that I stayed on when other chefs left in despair. The work was exacting but the guidance was fair – one great lesson that I have always remembered. Henri Dessibourg and I still keep in touch, exchanging the occasional letter and postcard.

A World of Experience

To travel and to see the many ways in which food is prepared, to be able to distinguish the good from the bad, the original and the exciting, is to understand the enjoyment that can be gained from one of life's necessities. From the very beginning I recognised that I had to learn the basics of the profession. It is these basic methods of preparation that form the multiplication tables of cookery. Without a comprehensive, practical understanding of elementary culinary skills it is not possible to progress. As I worked in the kitchen I would look out and notice guests arriving in cars – young men driving impressive, open-topped cars with beautiful women at their sides. The ambition to have a fine car and to escort a beautiful girl made me work even harder. Not many years passed before I bought a red, E-type Jaguar.

Monsieur Dessibourg arranged for me to spend the summer in Rome at the Cavalieri Hilton. Then I went back to Switzerland, to Sils-Maria where I was *commis saucier* in the Waldhaus.

Work took me to Canada for three years, to Montreal and the Queen Elizabeth Hotel. There I worked for one of the best men I have ever met – Albert Schnell. He was a wonderful human being. Albert's kitchens were highly organised. He saw some potential in my knowledge and promoted me to the position of his first assistant, in charge of 165 cooks, when I was only twenty-one. The experience was tremendous: I remember having to prepare a banquet for five thousand guests.

During Expo 67 I accepted a part-time job at the Canadian pavilion where all the official celebrations were held and lunches were served to royalty, presidents and ministers. I shared a room with a colleague who had undertaken the same

The end of my apprenticeship and my first season as an eighteen-year-old *commis de cuisine* at the Palace Hotel.

task. In the afternoon we rushed back to the hotel to work until eleven thirty.

After Canada I received lots of offers from hotels around the world but I knew that I was too young to accept a position as head chef. I wanted to go back to Switzerland for more training and above all to work for the head chef's diploma.

From Canada I went to Montreux, to another Palace Hotel, to work for Franz Wild who became a very good friend. Franz taught me the most about the head chef's diploma. He arranged for me to spend the winter season at the Palace Hotel in St Moritz under the leadership of eighty-seven year old Monsieur Defrance. Monsieur Defrance had spent part of his career working for Auguste Escoffier and, although he was eccentric and very fond of champagne, he was a great personality. As he worked in his office, Monsieur Defrance would frequently fall asleep over his papers and on many such occasions I gently shut the door to give him some peace. The *sous chef* (the chef's first assistant by the name of Cola, a splendid man and a great cook) would scream out orders and maintain control. In two hours three hundred meals had to be served, all under his frantic guidance. At the end of one such scrum, he put his arm around my shoulders and said, 'My dear son, you have done very well'. The *sous chef* felt very paternal after the rush. I once left my knives out during lunch and they disappeared. The chef collected knives to sell in Paris at the end of the season.

Japan

When I left Switzerland I had no idea just what a deep impression my next position was to have on me and on my cooking. In 1970 I applied for the post of *sous chef* at the Swiss pavilion for Expo 70 in Osaka. I was astonished but delighted, to be offered the position of head chef, a role that involved exercising

Above In 1970 I was offered the post of Executive Chef for the Swiss Pavilion at Expo 70 in Osaka, Japan and it was a wonderful experience.
Right Teaching plays a very important role in my career and I have taught all over the world. This is in the world-famous Tsuji School at Osaka in Japan.

leadership and management as well as culinary skills. My team consisted of thirty-five chefs of whom twenty-five were Japanese. The Japanese chefs were quick to learn, deft and beyond belief in terms of devotion. Even when quite ill they would come in to work – a practice I was quick to stop. I insisted that they would not lose face by staying away when they were ill.

Japan was a profound experience and there is still a lot of the Japanese influence left in me. I loved the life I led there and the attitude of the Japanese people. We western cooks can learn so much from the Japanese with regard to their desire for perfection and beauty in culinary art. During my time at Expo 70 I found a whole new vitality in culinary creation; I realised that the pleasures derived from a carefully prepared, aesthetically presented meal are joyful and unique experiences in their own right, with no need of any other justification.

The Japanese stay came to an end but the impression it made on me remains; the values that I encountered during the time I spent at Osaka are set firmly within me. It is sweetly significant that I have been back to Japan to teach them about Cuisine Naturelle. When I went back I was struck by my change in position: my previous visit had been one of learning; now I was teaching. My second visit served to refresh my memories of the Japanese people, their friendliness and politeness.

Five more posts as *chef de partie* followed Japan before I gained the head chef's diploma – the *Chef de Cuisine Diplôme* – at twenty-five, the youngest chef ever to do so. I worked hard to achieve that goal and I am proud that I did so at the first attempt, and at such a young age.

Then I came to London, to The Dorchester where I was asked to take up the role of first *sous chef* under Eugène Käufeler, *Maître Chef des Cuisines* for twenty-

Above Preparing a table of desserts for the sweet trolley at the Dorchester.
Right A selection of Cuisine Naturelle dishes: Steamed Halibut with Two Sauces, Poached Fillet of Beef with Crudités, Poached Scallops, Fruit Terrine, and Almond Basket with Raspberry Sauce.

five years. Even though I had never been to London before, I accepted the position without a moment's hesitation or a second thought because I knew that I would like working in that celebrated hotel.

The Dorchester

In November 1976 I succeeded Eugène Käufeler, taking responsibility for the kitchens and the cuisine at The Dorchester. This was something that I had always hoped for – to be given the opportunity of controlling the kitchens of a world-renowned hotel.

I will never forget my first day at The Dorchester. One of my *sous chefs* came to me and told me that he had a son who was just one year older than I was. He was a pleasant man, a small rather rounded figure, but I got the message. I knew that he could well end up disliking me. All one hundred and thirty two cooks joined the union because they felt insecure. They saw me as a young Swiss man, moving in to preside over chefs who had worked in the kitchens for twenty, thirty or forty years. It was not an easy role to fill and at first it was a very difficult job. My determination and ambition drove me on and prevented me from giving up in those early days. Every morning I shook hands with every member of my brigade and I would look for a happy response. If a person could not greet me happily, looking me straight in the eyes, I wanted to know why and I was concerned that any problems should be overcome. I wanted everyone to be content in their work, so I got to know each individual – who they were, their likes and dislikes, whether they were married and details of their families. I knew all the chefs' wives' names and I took a genuine pleasure in hearing about their homes. A year later only seven chefs remained in the union.

Above For me this captures a very happy time that merits the smile – at the Dorchester I had just been awarded a second star in the Michelin Guide.

Right Another proud moment in my career: I received the award for Chef of the Year 1985, presented by Caterer and Hotelkeeper magazine.

SPECIALITE DU CHEF

Above One of fifteen cartoons drawn by George Roland to commemorate the opening of Mosimann's.
Right With Udo Schlentrich, the general manager of The Dorchester, tasting a new creation.

Some time after joining The Dorchester I took a team of four chefs to a culinary exhibition in Germany and among them I included the *sous chef* who had approached me on my first day. Though he was the oldest member of the team, I took him because he had put so much work into The Dorchester. He had devoted a great part of his life to his job and this was intended as a small 'thank you'. Afterwards, as we stood on the stage receiving our gold medals at the exhibition, he was clearly moved by the experience and he was a happy man. He once told me that whenever he goes to the pub he wears the gold medal.

Not only did my approach to my staff bring about a significant change, also my approach to food was a bit radical. I introduced a lighter menu and all food was freshly cooked; it was to be an altogether more important feature of the hotel. Previously it was standard practice for guests to stay in the hotel and to eat elsewhere, but we changed that. With rebuilt kitchens we were in an even stronger position and after two years we won our first Michelin star. Two years later we received our second star: the only hotel restaurant outside France to be awarded two Michelin stars. I am still very proud of that.

There are too many tremendous memories to recount but one that stands out was preparing meals for Lord McAlpine, who entertained in a private dining room at the hotel three times a week. Each main course was named after the guest of honour and never did I repeat a menu. The Dorchester became the high spot of London – the Terrace Restaurant and Grill Room won the restaurant of the year award – and many celebrities dined there. Another culinary marathon, set deep in memory, was the preparation for the launch of *The French Cookery* series for *The Observer* when I prepared twenty six different soufflés, all to be served

Above A rare picture without my chef's hat and a moment of rest in a hectic day.
Right Sharing the knowledge and skills that I have acquired always gives me great pleasure.

simultaneously. Each letter of the alphabet was represented by a soufflé – apple, banana, *champignon* and so on – not one letter missed and each soufflé perfect.

We reached a point when the restaurant was so well booked that residents could not be guaranteed a table. My favourite joke at the time was that customers had to be asked please to book a table in the restaurant first, then to book the room. It was in fact true.

We had over six hundred and fifty applicants on a waiting list for a position in the kitchens. They were young chefs from all over the world, eager to learn and expand their knowledge of cooking. How did I select them? Not by religion race, age or sex. My chief concern was that they should have the right attitude and that they were keen to learn. I looked for people who couldn't wait to get up in the morning because they loved their work. Of my staff at The Dorchester, eighty-five per cent were British and the others were from all over the world. I called them my children and I treated them as I would my family: I think I was hard but fair and spent hours sorting out their personal problems or advising on their careers. I took a real interest in their future careers. Today many of the chefs who trained in my kitchens hold key positions in restaurants and hotels all over the world: I am the culinary father of many.

To be a chef you have not only to be interested in cooking, you must love it. To lead a team of chefs who are happy in their work, who are giving all they have to their work and who are capable of learning all the time, you have to like people – and I do. I have worked in kitchens where knives flew, where voices were always raised and where fear was a daily presence. Not for me – I tried to make sure that the right people were put into the right jobs so that their own talents came to the

Above Pigs are trained for truffle hunting in Perigord. I am led off by an enthusiastic pig.
Top right With my two boys, Philipp and Mark, on an early-morning expedition to Billingsgate Market. They are fascinated by the live lobster but just a little cautious.
Bottom right The BBC sent me off to Sheffield to cook Sunday lunch for John Willcock's family of six for under £10.00. I see what Sheffield Market has to offer.

fore. The chef's profession demands a single-minded approach, almost holy devotion. Success depends on perfection in the smallest details and this was the message I offered my brigade in those hot but happy kitchens.

More Than a Little Learning

There is always something new to learn – why shouldn't I continue my own education? I learn something every day. At every stage in my career I have looked for the new things that I ought to be learning, sometimes not in obvious areas. I never ask anyone to do anything that I cannot, or would not, do myself. In the early days I took courses on diet and on flambé work to learn about the subjects I felt were my weakest. Before I went to The Dorchester I spent a winter season at the Palace Hotel in Gstaad as a *commis pâtissier* because I really felt that my experience with pâtisserie was not as extensive as it could be. I enjoyed the time there, I learnt a lot and I extended my basic skills. I have taken other courses in areas related to my work, for example in teaching and management. The courses, the experience, the hard work and the people have all helped and I love to encourage anyone else who is prepared to work and to learn.

At The Dorchester I set up weekly training courses and actively encouraged everyone to participate. In the kitchen with my staff, I have always seen my own role as leading, guiding and advising them as well as learning and developing my own ideas and skills. We are never beyond learning. I have always wanted to motivate others – I need action and I love to organise.

In our profession it is vital to learn the basics: how to poach, how to grill, how to braise. Basic methods do not change from country to country: if you cook in Sydney, New York or London they are the same. All the people who worked with

me were taught this basic knowledge. Why does milk boil over? What makes a soufflé rise? An understanding of these facts of the science of food makes the whole process of cooking far easier.

Moving On

After thirteen happy, successful, and good years at The Dorchester it was time to move on. After all, during that time we had five different owners and ten managers. Among them were some of the best managers that I have ever worked with. Why did I decide that it was time to leave?

I wanted to cook for friends, for people I know and like. I had offers – very good offers – from all over the world for managerial positions, head chef posts or other opportunities. I could have opened a restaurant in London. No. I wanted to do something different; I wanted to create something unique in the way of a dining club. I was lucky to find the church premises, already converted into a club and it was a challenge for me to change the old interior and make it special.

Here I have found a new focus for my philosophy of food, where I can share my cuisine. It is exhilarating to cook for people I know, to take into account their likes and dislikes; it is like having an extremely large family. For me there is nothing nicer than seeing people enjoying themselves, having a good time during and after their meal. You must love people before you can serve them and this is something that I have never forgotten.

I want to celebrate the delights and pleasures of eating food that is light and wholesome yet looks irresistible – this is my aim for my club. Every morning I look forward to doing something different or better. It's essential in my profession to deliver every day – I did something good today, I have to do it at least as well

again tomorrow. I am proud to be a perfectionist. The chef's profession is one of the few in which you do not get a second chance.

Good Food and Good Living

If you are a chef, your livelihood depends on giving pleasure to other people. We are creative, though what we create is gone almost instantly. There is always the thought that perhaps tomorrow you will do it even better. One needs to have simple confidence in oneself. Someone who wants to please has a tendency to do too much. The raw materials produced by nature are in themselves the finest food.

If moderate amounts of food – the best seasonal vegetables and fruit, the most beautiful fish, the leanest slices of meat and the least fatty of dairy produce – are prepared with delicacy and eaten with wholehearted appreciation then the result is that we are in better temper, of more active mind and far healthier in body. This approach promotes a happiness of spirit, balanced both mentally and physically. Good food and good living go hand in hand.

I read one day that 35,000 people die of heart attacks every year in Britain, and I asked myself 'What can I do to help?'. Diet, after all, is the nub of the matter. For so many years, chefs have been seen as the least innovative within the area of healthy eating. Healthy eating need not be at the expense of fine food. That is why I created Cuisine Naturelle. I work closely with The Family Heart Association to encourage other chefs to share my interest in food that is light and wholesome.

I think it is because I have devoted myself to work and because I genuinely love food and cooking, that people have come to show an interest in what I do. For me, concentrating on, enjoying and loving my cooking is very important. At the same time, I find that many people are eager to learn about Cuisine Naturelle, of the

Above I have never lost my love of sports and I relax by jogging for three to four miles most mornings.
Right When they can – at weekends or during the school holidays – my boys join me in my morning jog.

Not a bottle to be seen. Crystal decanters are the only vessels on display behind the bar at Mosimann's.

simplicity and subtlety that are the rules of my cooking. I in turn am learning the ways in which I can communicate with readers, or through the medium of television to viewers.

We have all come to expect artistry in cooking as well as in other aspects of life. When a meal is laid out artistically, when your guests look at the plate and cannot wait to eat, this is when food is truly appetising. To cook really well, one must have a feeling for that certain ingredient that may be missing. For me, cooking has become an art. Before I begin to cook, I particularly enjoy thinking about the food, imagining the flavour combinations and mentally preparing the dish. I choose colours; I mix sweet and sour; I feel my way through, trying to find something new; then I relax and it suddenly comes to me. Beautiful!

Food and cooking are my art and my art is the means I have of communicating with people.

When I participate in campaigns for healthy eating, judging competitions and offering ideas, I am always glad to see the talented young people who are ready to learn and I am eager to inspire them to work for their future.

Mosimann's

The change from being employed to taking on the club is both a challenge and a new opportunity. The fact that the club is called 'Mosimann's' is significant: I want to make this a place where I can share my ideas and culinary standards with all the members.

When I first moved in, I took time to get to know the club as it was then, to get to know the members and to sort out my own ambitions for the establishment. I spent a great deal of time working on the ideas for the refurbishment before I decided that I could go ahead with the work. Then I felt happy and inspired to begin the major task and the hard work which it involved.

I am proud of the club – there are so many features that are unique and designed specifically to please the clientele. Members have the opportunity to visit the glass-fronted wine store which is stocked with unusual, special wines. I love the bar, where instead of bottles there are crystal decanters, and I know that everyone who relaxes there appreciates the special surroundings.

The old club was changed in three months, from the kitchen to the top floor. At first nobody would believe that it was possible; but we did it. Every single day I was there, in my overalls, talking to everyone and encouraging them in their work. I appreciated the skills of the builders, the patience of the person who was stripping all the woodwork, and the craft of the carpenters. They all became friends during their time spent renovating the club and I promised them all a meal with their wives or partners if they could get all the work finished by my hard deadline. I used the carrot not the stick; and it worked.

On one day, while the work was in progress, I had to go to New York – just for the day – but when I came back I really felt that I had been missed. People had asked where the 'old man' was.

As well as the restaurant area, there are private rooms set aside for functions; designed for different types of gatherings. Each one offers a particular ambience that is unique to the club. Now that the club is established, I want it to stay ahead, and I am always looking for opportunities and ways of improving existing systems or creating new features. The freedom that comes with being your own boss is something which I am just beginning to appreciate and I intend to use it to the

With Marques, the wine waiter at Mosimann's, discussing and selecting wines in the specially designed wine cellar.

full. I would like to expand the culinary areas for which I am known as well as introduce new concepts. When occasions demand that I offer something extra, then I want to make sure that I am ready with the ideas.

After only six months we had an impressive list of distinguished members. Two kings had visited the club as well as many members of the British royal family. I am a very lucky man.

What Next?

Eating should be combined with fun and I think I have shown how we can eat extremely well, yet healthily at the same time. A healthy, happy person creates a desire in others for health and happiness.

The future? I love to work. Every morning I put on my chef's jacket and I feel proud to be a cook. Regrets? Never. Every day is wonderful – I repeat, I feel proud every time I put on my chef's jacket. To be ready to learn is vital.

I love teaching. Every year I go to Lausanne to the famous hotel school for four or five days to teach kitchen management and the rudiments of motivation. It is important to appreciate what other people are doing for you.

I derive enormous pleasure from travelling and learning about other people's attitudes. I remember my time in Italy, when I worked with Italians, stayed with them, lived with them and got to know them. One problem that is so often evident is that we do not learn enough of the attitudes of different peoples. Remember, if you are working with people of a different culture, then make the effort to get to know them; your efforts will be greatly appreciated.

Over the years I have not lost my fascination for cars. That first crush on the Chevrolet and my own-topped Spitfire sowed the seeds of a future hobby. I have to

Above Kit Chan who has worked with me for eight years and supported me on many promotional trips all over the world.
Right Outside Mosimann's, my dining club, happy to be the proprietor of my own business.

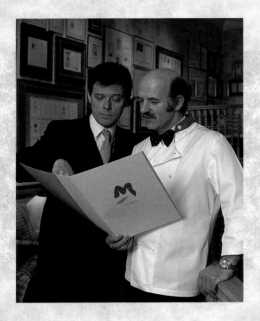

admit to being a great motoring enthusiast. I have always been a keen sportsman so it comes naturally to exercise regularly, to jog, play squash or swim. My more sedentary interest is collecting old cookery books and I have over four thousand in my library. I have housed them in the club so that others can share the pleasure which they give me.

A closing thought: the personality of the chef is his backbone and it is important that the backbone is not allowed to change as the body changes from year to year.

Above With John Davey, my restaurant
manager, discussing the menu for lunch.
Right Outside Mosimann's with my team.
Far right The end of a busy day.

MY ART

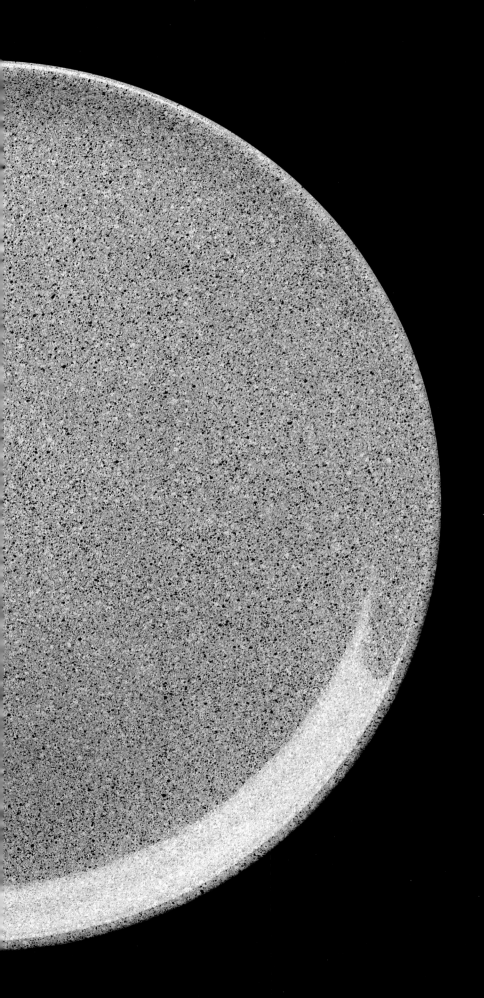

*I*f you are a chef, your life is devoted to giving pleasure to other people. We are creative, and what we create is gone almost instantly; but there is always the thought that maybe tomorrow we will create something even better.

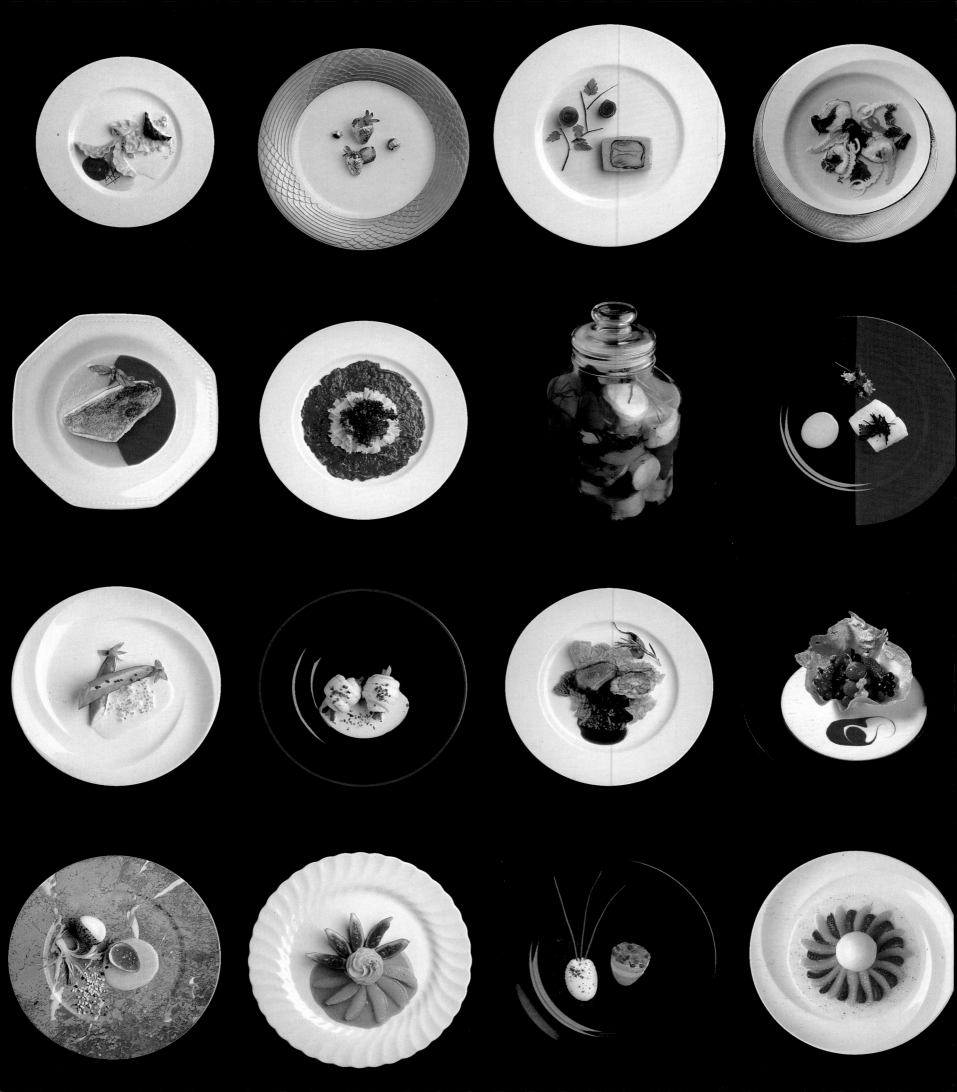

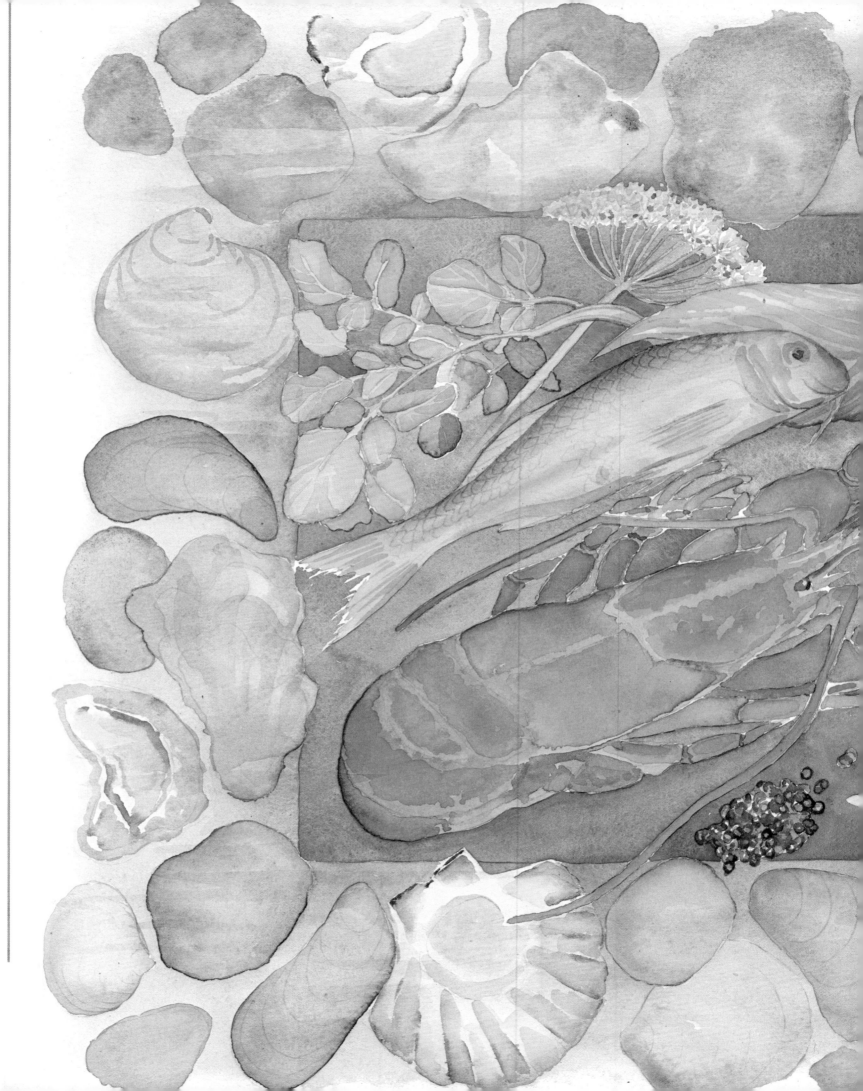

Fruits of the seas and rivers

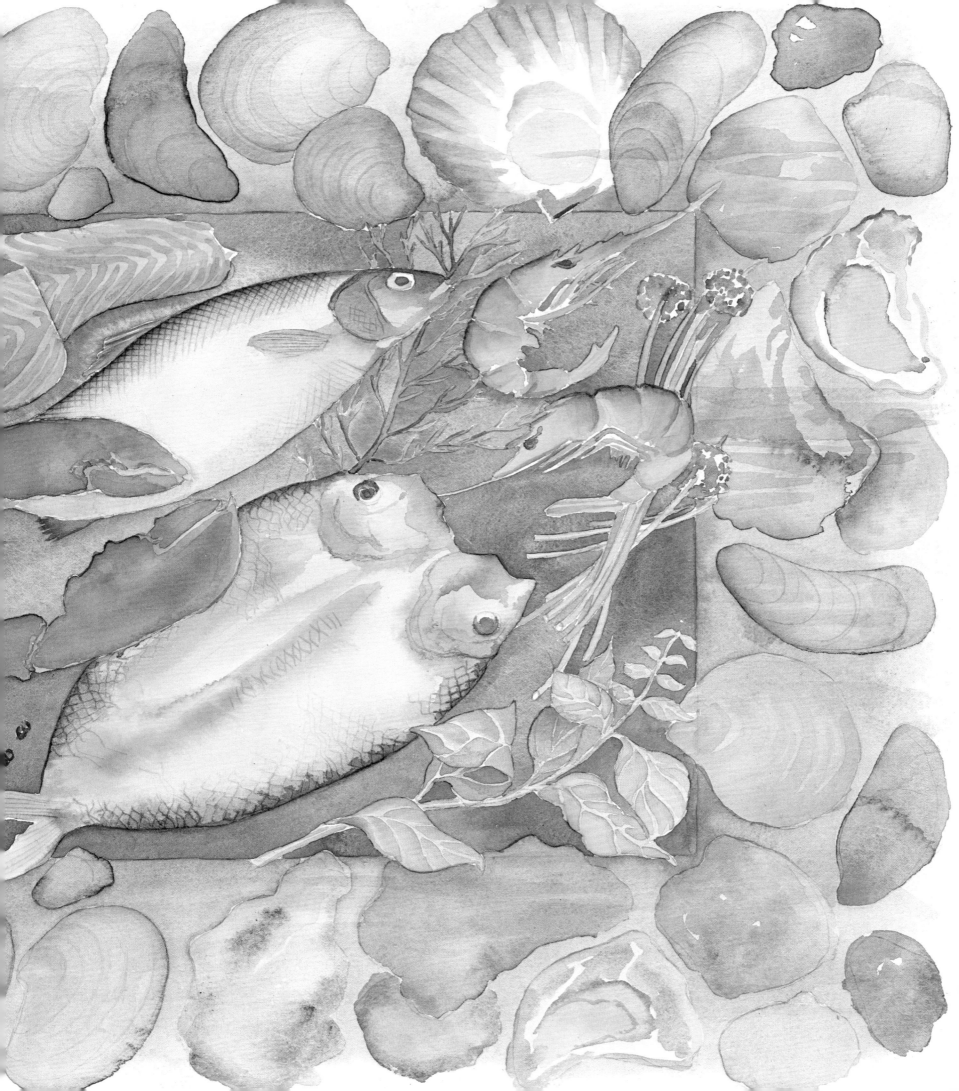

TURBOT FILLET

with curry sauce

TURBOT is one of the finest fish of the sea and it needs
little to accentuate its full glory. The plate and a spoonful
of sauce accentuate the pearliness of its white, dense flesh.

Marinated Salmon

with coriander and violets

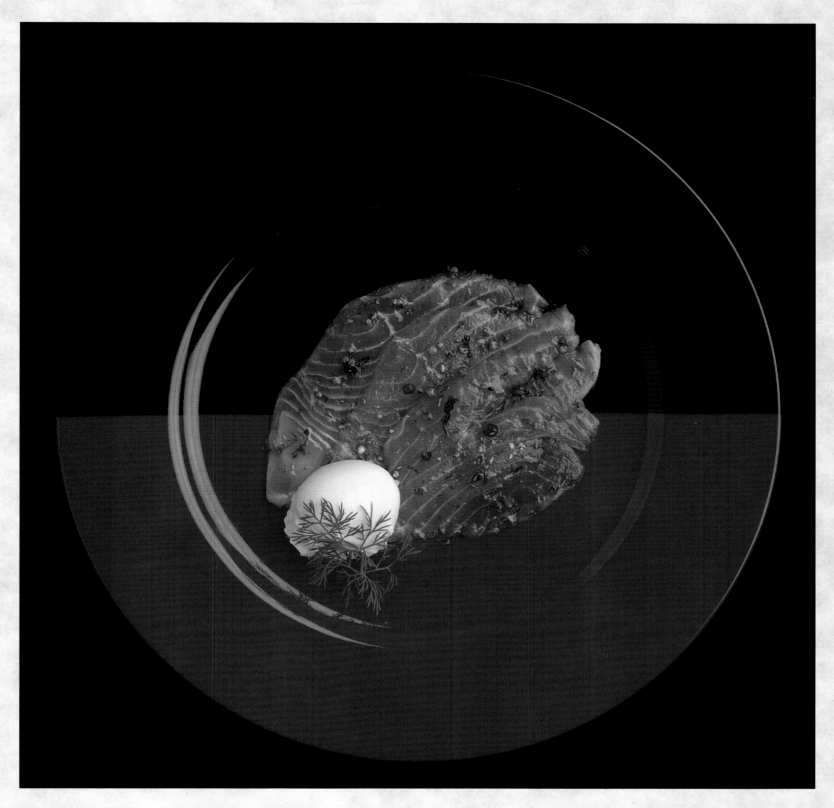

THE UTTER SIMPLICITY of this dish accentuates the
translucent nature of the salmon flesh and the perfection
of a softly poached egg.

GRILLED MONKFISH

in warm vinaigrette with coriander

*T*his perfectly grilled monkfish is ideal for
eating out of doors, on a vine-shaded terrace,
overlooking majestic olive groves, under a blue
cathedral of mistral-scoured sky.

A MELANGE of flavours – garlic, coriander and olive oil
combined with fresh chives, tarragon and basil – made for
a warm summer's day, to be enjoyed with
a cold bottle of wine.

SALMON TARTARE

with watercress sauce

FILLET OF SOLE

in a parsley crust with steamed oysters

THE PLEASING TEXTURE and fine flavour of wild Scottish salmon, marinated with a hint of dill and sharpened with lemon juice, are complemented by the watercress and enriched with beluga caviar.

STEAMING IS ONE of the finest cooking methods for seafood — it brings out the prized flavour of the sole, preserves the delicate texture of the fillets, and retains the juicy succulence of the tender oysters.

CHARCOAL-GRILLED FILLET OF RED MULLET

with saffron noodles

THE SUNNY, warm colour and smooth strands of these
saffron egg noodles make the perfect bed for the juices of
the succulent, grilled red mullet, scented with
a hint of basil.

KIPPER AND CREAM MOUSSELINE

with caviar

I HAVE ALWAYS LOVED the art of understatement
without meanness and this is often apparent in my dishes.
Here is a sublime combination of kipper mousse, richly
covered in a crust of caviar.

NEST OF COLOURED NOODLES

with sea bass

A NEST of coloured noodles is cheerful and uplifting to
the spirits and it forms a perfect setting for
this freshly baked bass, catching its juices as they
mingle with the cream sauce.

TWIN FILLETS OF RED MULLET

à la nage

THE BEAUTY of this dish lies in its complete simplicity
and yet every part of it has been carefully
prepared and specially chosen to complement the
unique, pink sheen of the mullet.

ROSETTE AND ROULADE OF SMOKED SALMON

with quark and chive mousse

IT IS IMPORTANT that every dish should be eye-catching
to ensure a pleasing first impression. A simple, light
mousse is enclosed in a covering of smoked salmon and
presented with the minimum of garnish.

GRILLED SCOTTISH SALMON

with ratatouille of Provençal vegetables

THE VERY NATURE of salmon flesh, with its thick fillets,
rich in natural juices, makes it ideal for grilling.
Here it is served with a bright ratatouille of tender,
diced vegetables.

CONSOMME OF
FRESHWATER CRAYFISH

BLACK-BANDED BREAM
with wild garlic and lemon balm

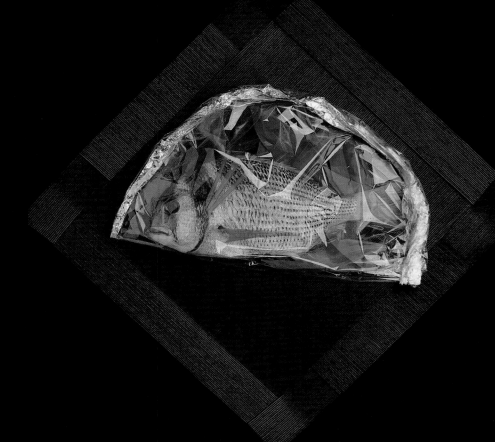

THE ESSENCE of this delicate and desirable creature is distilled into this lovely soup. The serenity and dark austerity of the table setting allows the soup the visual impact it deserves.

COOKING EN PAPILLOTE captures all the fragrance and flavoursome juices from the ingredients. Using a clear parcel enables one to see and enjoy the beauty of the fish and the aromatics.

SUSHI

Japan made a strong impression on me. I think that western cooks can learn a lot from the Japanese with regard to perfection and aestheticism in culinary art.

THE SHAPES, COLOURS AND TEXTURES that make up the pieces of sushi illustrate the artistic qualities of Japanese cooking. In making sushi, I indulge my special affection for seafood and the desire for perfection.

STEAMED LOBSTER

with fresh herbs

COLD LOBSTER has such a delicate flavour that
I always take care in choosing a salad to accompany it
from among the best, freshest and most
colourful of the market's produce.

LIGHTLY BOUND with an ivory wine sauce and
arranged with fresh, warmed salad leaves, this rendez-vous
of the freshest, choice seafood should taste clearly of
the ocean.

FRESHWATER CRAYFISH

with samphire

*S*amphire has been pickled by farmers' wives and sold in the village markets near Boulogne for years. In England it grows wild, especially on the east coast, and it is beginning to appear more regularly in the fishmonger's shops.

SAMPHIRE is juicy, aromatic and sometimes pungent, and it goes well with crustaceans. Here I serve it with that glorious, scarlet, little lobster of freshwater streams – the crayfish.

Symphonie de fruits
de mer et de terre

Steamed scallops
with a ratatouille of vegetables and sauce coraille

LAYING the seafood and fish on this vivid yellow sauce is like placing them against the eye of the sun. Turmeric is used to create a sauce that is unique in flavour as well as colour.

TO ACCENTUATE their sweet, satin tenderness, I have set these lightly steamed scallops on a simple ratatouille of ripe tomato, red, orange and yellow pepper, and chopped shallots.

HERE I PRESENT a lovely variation of the seafood
cocktails served in a brilliant consommé on the opposite
page. This time, the finest ingredients are gathered on a
black plate with a fine red rim.

THIS IS refreshing and voluptuous at the same time.
The richness of choice of the exquisite fruits de mer is in
contrast to the lightness and clarity of the
surrounding jellied bouillon.

*T*he luminous nacre of the concave oyster shell is as visually arresting as the craggy cover which protects the sweet, meaty flesh within. Here I serve a fine oyster with a small young lemon, and its fragrant lime-scented leaves, so that the wonder of this creature's salty tang of the sea may be enjoyed in pure simplicity.

Oyster Rock

with lemon

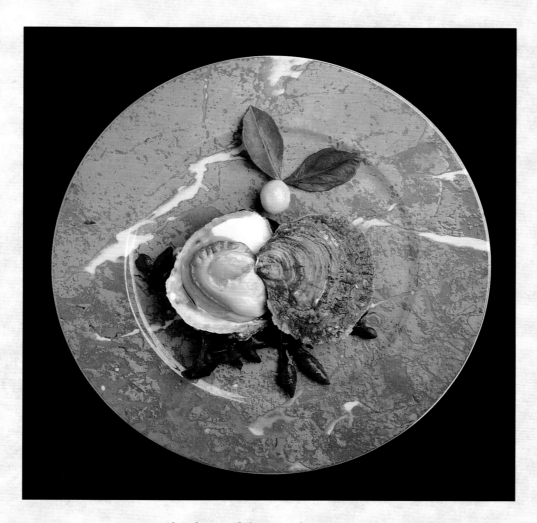

WHEN I SAW this beautiful stone-finished plate, it seemed
so like the ocean-washed rocks from which oysters
were gathered, that I knew it would make the perfect
background for this succulent Colchester native.

From the land and air

SPICED CHICKEN LIVER PARFAIT

with tomato roses

THIS IS ONE of my favourite dishes in the book
and its dramatic presentation on this black and red plate
is as lively as the flavour.

YELLOW is one of the sunniest of colours and it makes a
cheering start to a meal, especially when presented on this
unusual black and white plate.

SAUCISSE DE LEGUMES

suprême de caille grillé

*H*ere the saucisse de légumes is cooked
with a breast of quail over a small brazier in which
the glowing charcoal has died to ash-grey.

THE COLOURFUL vegetable sausage curves gently
around the breast of the quail and they are both grilled
over charcoal – perhaps one of the most
aromatic ways of cooking.

WARM CHICKEN

with Japanese salad

BREAST OF CHICKEN

on broccoli cream sauce with julienne vegetables

THIS DISH is excellent to start a meal of many courses. Delicate chicken, with the simple salad, is light and appetising, awakening the appetite and pleasing the eye.

THE SUCCULENCE of this lovely dish is derived from the steamed chicken served on a richer broccoli sauce. Glace de volaille, marbled through the sauce, emphasises the chicken flavour.

*T*he good cook loves and enjoys his work, and
all good cooks have in common both the desire
and capacity to produce something really first
rate. There has never been a more exciting
time to cook.

STEAMED BABY CHICKEN

on pine needles

STEAMING is one of my favourite ways of cooking. One can choose from many fragrances to perfume the steam and thereby suffuse the little chicken with aromatics while rendering it moist and succulent.

DISHES SUCH as this remind me of the origins of English
cooking. The cauldron was used to boil the puddings, the
fowls and vegetables, and the wonderful broth sustained
the family and farm workers alike.

MOUSSELINE OF CHICKEN LIVER

with raspberry coulis

THE FINEST of chicken liver mousselines, delicately
flavoured with a hint of mixed spice and allspice, is served
with a tart, fruity coulis of fresh raspberries and garnished
with salad leaves.

POACHED FILLET OF BEEF

with horseradish vinaigrette

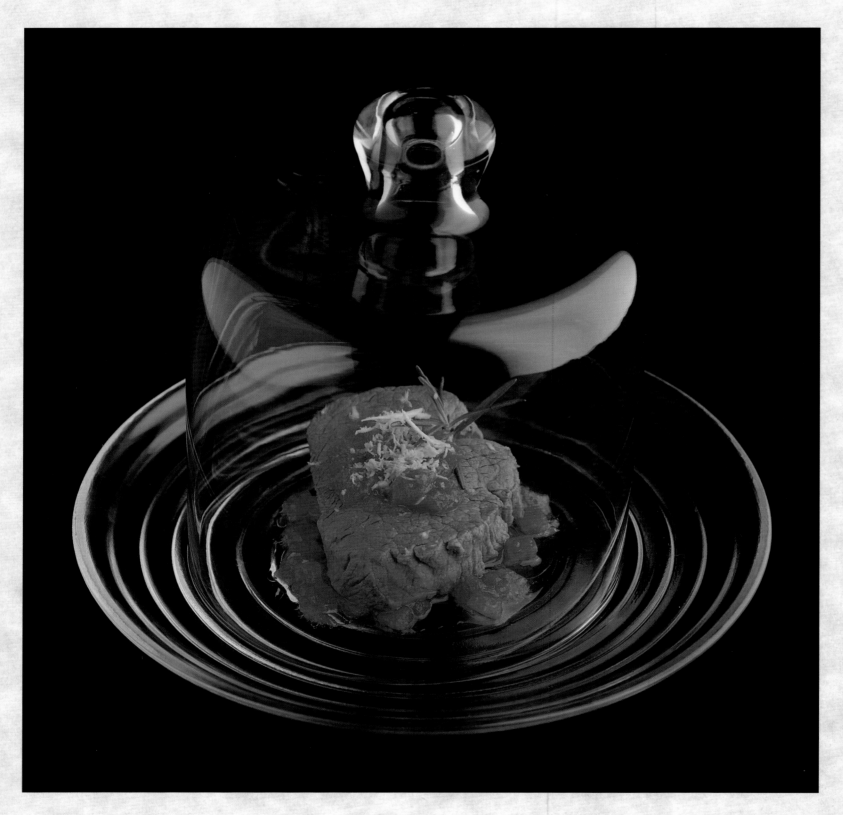

ENCLOSED and reflected in a beautiful crystal plate and
cloche, this fillet of beef keeps warm, while
absorbing the flavours of the clear sauce as it is
served to guests.

HORS D'OEUVRE OF SALMON CAVIAR

and elixir of beef

THIS SMALL BOWL of salmon caviar will uplift your
spirits at the start of the meal. Sample the magic of its
shining, moist transparency and butterfly-wing-thin crust,
flavoured with the sweet-salt juice of the ocean.

SWEETBREAD SOLO

with tomato coulis

THE PALE, HUMBLE SWEETBREAD, transformed to a
golden delicacy, is served with a refreshing coulis of
tomato, then garnished with a cherry tomato and a curled
spring onion.

ROAST RACK OF LAMB

with wild mushrooms and roasted shallots

A **TENDER RACK** of lamb is roasted
to pink perfection, glazed with a glossy brown sauce
and served with shallots roasted
in their skins.

CARPACCIO

with a ruffle of cheese

THE EXHILARATING colour of carpaccio contrasts nicely
with the tender creamy curls of *Tête de Moine* – a
cylindrical Swiss cheese – which is shaved off in a ruffle by
using a small circular knife.

Welsh Mountain Lamb

with truffle and herb crust

ALTHOUGH I AM ALWAYS INTERESTED in the new
influences in cooking, there are times when I return to the
simple dishes which we have cooked in Europe for decades.
However, I may present the dish in a different way.

GULL'S EGG SERVED ON A WATERCRESS SAUCE

with salmon caviar

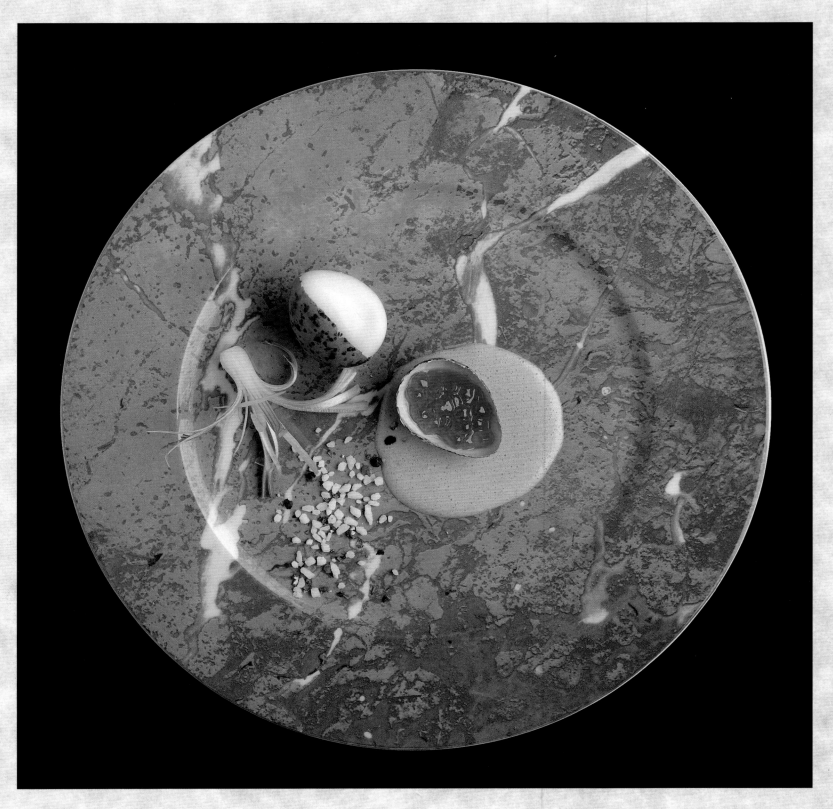

THE ROCK-LIKE finish of this plate brings
together the beginnings of life found in sea, in streams
and on the edges of the breakers.

LEEK TERRINE

with trompettes de morte

IN THIS TERRINE all the nuances of colour
are brought out. The leeks are pressed together
and held by nothing other than their juices.

QUAIL'S EGG

with caviar

There is such beauty in food and ingredients
that I am constantly refreshed and excited.
Just look at this lightly fried egg in perfect
miniature, with its sunny yolk and tender white,
served with a large spoonful of caviar. The grains
are so large, one can feel them bursting
in one's mouth.

THIS STUNNING photograph illustrates that simplicity
and restraint often produce the greatest impact – a perfect
example of 'less is more'.

SCRAMBLED EGGS

with caviars

ACQUA D'ORO

HERE I SERVE three fresh farm eggs, lightly scrambled
with a scrap of butter and cream, in their shells and
crowned with the royal eggs from the sea.

I HAVE ALWAYS enjoyed making this clear quail soup.
The flavour of quail is most satisfying, especially when
concentrated into sparkling consommé.

SALADE DE POMMES D'AMOUR

au citron vert

THESE CHERRY TOMATOES glow like jewels in
a pool on this dark bed of samphire.

A MOUSSE of carrot, turnip and broccoli, with a
colourful garnish, is scooped into perfect portions.

*T*omatoes make one of the most successful of all
mousses: their appetising coral colour,
their sweet and refreshing flavour, and their welcome
note of acidity together make a desirable
start to a meal.

RENDEZ-VOUS DE POMMES D'AMOUR

ON THIS PLATE I have assembled a slice from
a terrine of tomatoes, a coquille of tomato mousse, and
a yellow tomato.

TIMBALE FLORENTINE

with saffron sauce

DARK, RICH SPINACH makes an excellent purée to
flavour a light savoury custard. Set in the spinach-lined
mould, the timbale is served with a golden saffron sauce,
flecked with saffron, and garnished with carrot.

TRUFFLES WRAPPED IN RAVIOLI

in a chicken consommé

I LOVE the stark contrast in this dish: the
humble ravioli filled with the truffles – the black diamonds
of the Perigord – garnishing this clear and excellently
flavoured soup.

MANGE TOUT

stuffed with a vegetable mousseline

THE **SIMPLE ELEGANCE** of the smooth shape of the
mange tout, filled with the mousseline stuffing and
enriched with nuggets of vegetable dice, is as lovely to
look at as it is good to eat.

THIS TERRINE, made either of yellow or red
peppers, seems to hold all the sunshine in which they were
ripened, both in the tender, colourful flesh, in the vivid
sauce and in the clear jelly.

WHEN YOU have some freshly cooked carrots to
hand you may like to try out this little timbale of two
mousselines. The brilliance of their colours is
highlighted by the lustrous plate.

LES PETITS LEGUMES

à la Grecque

BY POURING a warm vinaigrette over a dish of
vegetables, and allowing them time to absorb the flavour,
a recipe of new dimensions is created to add to the
usual selection of leafy salads on the cold table.

SAUCISSE DE LEGUMES

sauce aux fèves

SET IN the soft sweetness of celeriac mousse,
the crisp and delicious vegetables can be seen dimly, as
through a veil, giving one a glimpse of the surprises
and excitement beneath.

NEW POTATOES

with beluga caviar

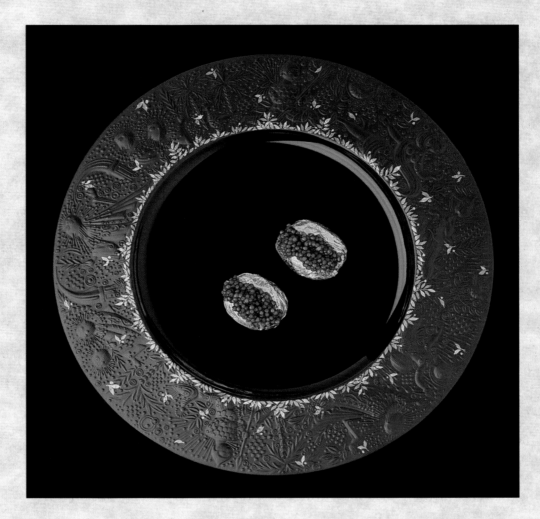

WHEN I SAW this very unusual, fantasy plate it
gave me the background for this idea which is a
wonderful combination of the poorest and
richest ingredients.

Fruits of the earth

MANGO ON BLACKBERRY VELVET

IT IS DESIRABLE that some desserts are vibrantly
coloured to make the necessary impact after several fine
courses of a meal. This is a beautiful example – the colours
are dramatic but the dessert itself is light and refreshing.

POACHED PEAR

served with crème à l'Anglaise of caramel and chocolate

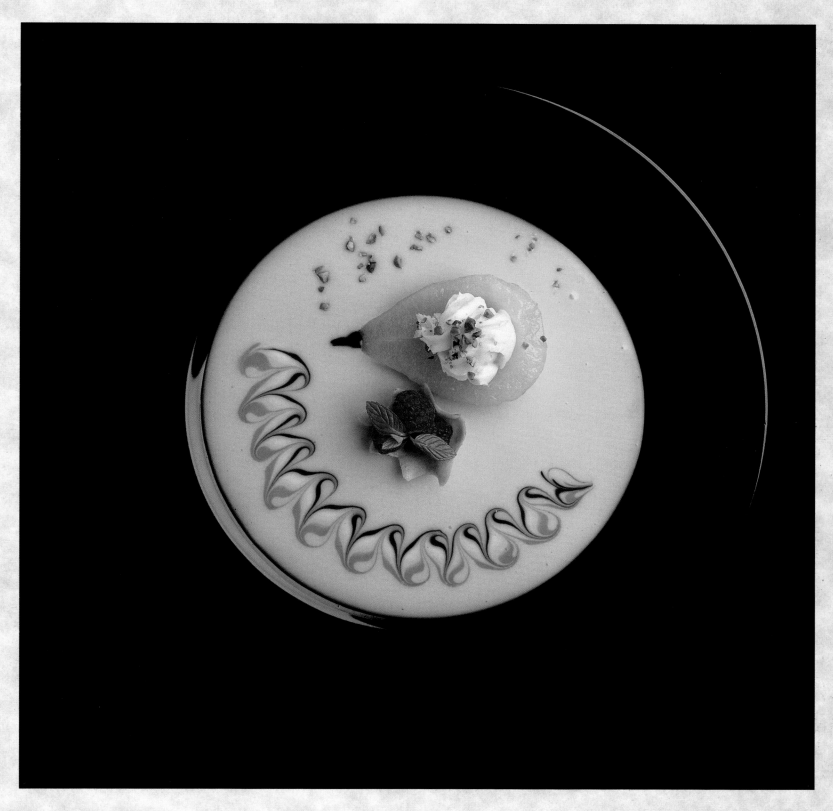

AUTUMN-RIPENED pears are cooled in an orange-
flavoured poaching syrup until golden and glossy. The
contrasting textures and flavours of pistachio ice cream
and crisp biscuit complete the dessert.

AN ENGLISH SUMMER PUDDING

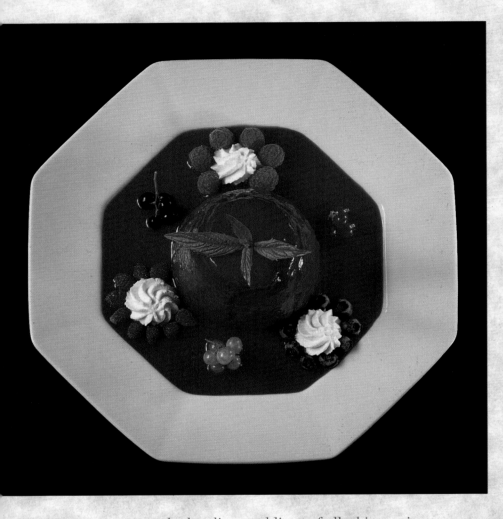

I mould the pudding with the minimum of bread, using just a few leaves of gelatine to keep its tender shape.

ONE OF the loveliest puddings of all: this one is drenched in the jewel-dark juices of the soft fruit, picked at the height of their summer ripeness when they are bursting with flavour.

STRAWBERRY STAR

with oranges

RHUBARB SORBET

in almond flowers

STRAWBERRIES and oranges complement each other beautifully in colour, tartness and sweetness. Here I have arranged them in a sunburst of red and gold, with a lime syrup and a smooth, vanilla ice cream.

I PARTICULARLY ENJOY making a beautiful dish from a simple fruit or vegetable. Here I have taken a compôte of rhubarb, with its delicious tart flavour, and made it into a delicate pink sorbet.

YOGHURT-CREAMED OATS

with blueberries and apple

THIS GOBLET holds the secret to health and vitality,
designed to be taken with the tonic of Swiss mountain air,
the scent of Alpine meadow flowers, and against a
background of expanses of clear blue Engadiner skies.

MELON makes one of the best sorbets of all: the sweet
penetrating perfume and luscious flesh give the sorbet a
softness and roundness that is not found in
sorbets made from other fruits.

THIS IS ONE of the most luscious of all chocolate
creations – a mousse of rich bitter chocolate,
with a mousse of softer, sweeter, white chocolate nestling
nearby, both on three different chocolate sauces:
white, milk and dark.

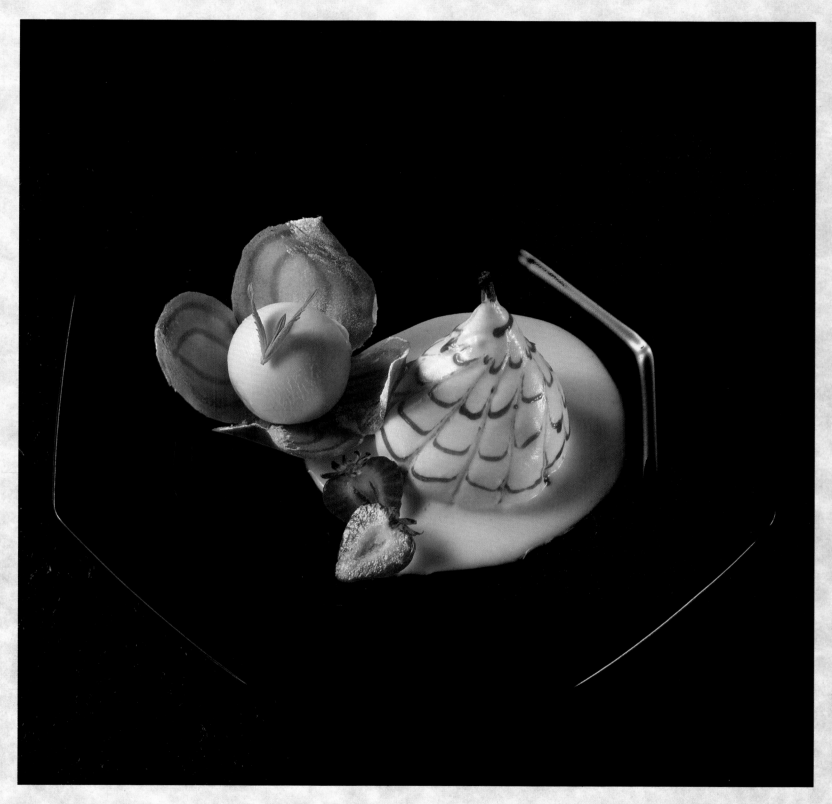

THE PERFECT heart shape of the strawberry is
reflected throughout this dessert – even the almond-flavoured
biscuit orchid, which embraces the saffron
ice cream, repeats the tender and appealing outline
of the fruit.

STRAWBERRY SWAN LAKE

Swans gliding with proud serenity on Swiss lakes were so much a part of my childhood that I have a particular affection for them.

THIS ENCHANTING dessert is made from meringue, filled with sliced English strawberries and crème chantilly, then served with a creamy vanilla sauce.

CHOCOLATE AND ORANGE

cream mousse

SNOW EGGS

with caramel cobwebs

THE COMBINATION of chocolate and orange is a
wonderfully sensual one and I have tried to accentuate this
by making the chocolate very dark and very smooth.
The orange gives the right refreshing balance.

THIS IS A classic dessert in which the lightly
sweetened snow eggs are poached in milk and served with
a creamy, vanilla sauce, then decorated with
golden caramel threads.

WHEN STRAWBERRIES and raspberries are abundant in
the garden, and blackberries grow wild and sweet in the
hedgerows, make a tall cooler of these berry fruits mixed
with their exotic cousins from other lands.

THE LIGHTEST SUGAR SYRUP and a selection of fruit
make up the rainbow colours in this crushed ice refresher.
For serving between courses of a meal, it has a clearer,
less-sweet flavour than the usual sorbet.

PARFAIT OF GRAND MARNIER

with passion fruit sauce

THIS DESSERT is based on a smooth, frozen parfait,
carefully flavoured with Grand Marnier. The crisp frilled
biscuit cups; clear, golden passion-fruit sauce;
and tiny hearts of raspberry sauce complete the
summery creation.

BAKED BANANAS

with fruit in foil

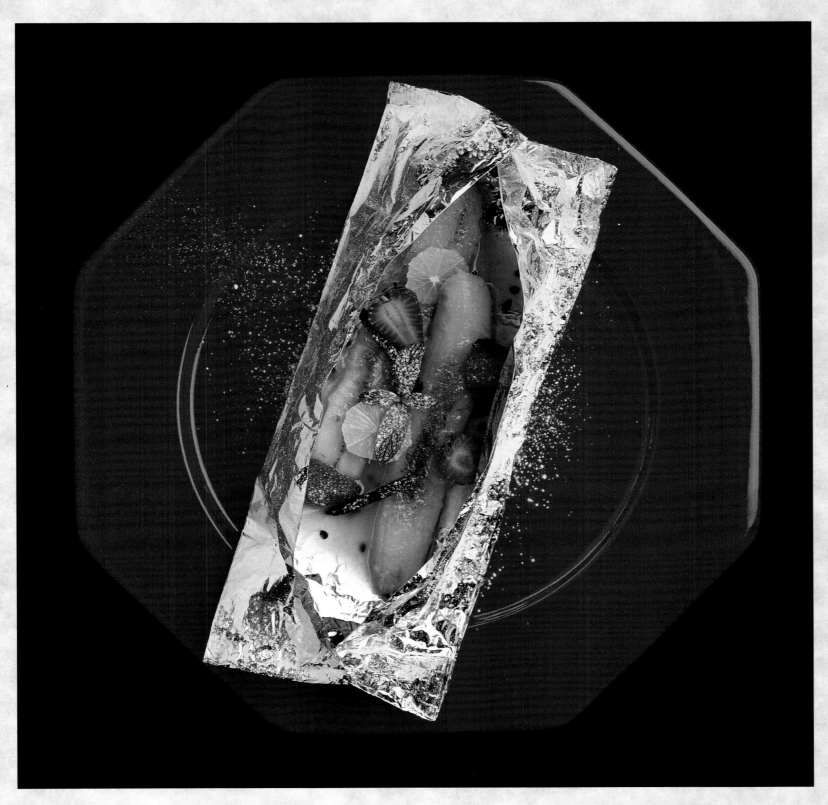

THERE ARE SO MANY BEAUTIFUL FRUITS that it is a
pleasure to create light desserts. Ripe bananas, zesty citrus
fruits and exotic passion fruits are baked in neatly
sealed pouches to release their combined aromas as the
package is opened.

GILDED BERRY JEWELS

THESE SPLENDID FRUITS make a glorious combination
— a raspberry, blueberry and strawberries in gold leaf
arranged on this gorgeous plate, the pattern which
surrounds them like the feathers of a golden bird.

PARFAIT OF RASPBERRIES AND VANILLA

THE FLAVOURS of this iced parfait are echoed in the
sauce and the decoration. This creates a delightful contrast
in the taste – the raspberries are presented in three ways:
fresh, frozen and in a velvety purée.

CHOCOLATE MOUSSE

with white and dark chocolate sauces

DARK AND DEVILISH, an irresistible creation
that allows sheer indulgence in all three types of chocolate
— from the finest and darkest bitter
chocolate to the smoothest, creamy, white chocolate
— presented with a glossy sauce.

FIG SORBET

with fresh figs and oranges

THE PLAIN, OUTER APPEARANCE of the fresh fig
blossoms into beauty as the fruit is cut open and its rich,
deep colour when fully ripe is matched by its sweetness.
Flavoured with cinnamon, this vibrant sorbet is served
with a zesty sauce of orange.

SCALLOPS of pear, grilled until tender and caramelised to
intensify their flavour, lie between these fine sheets
of almond pastry.

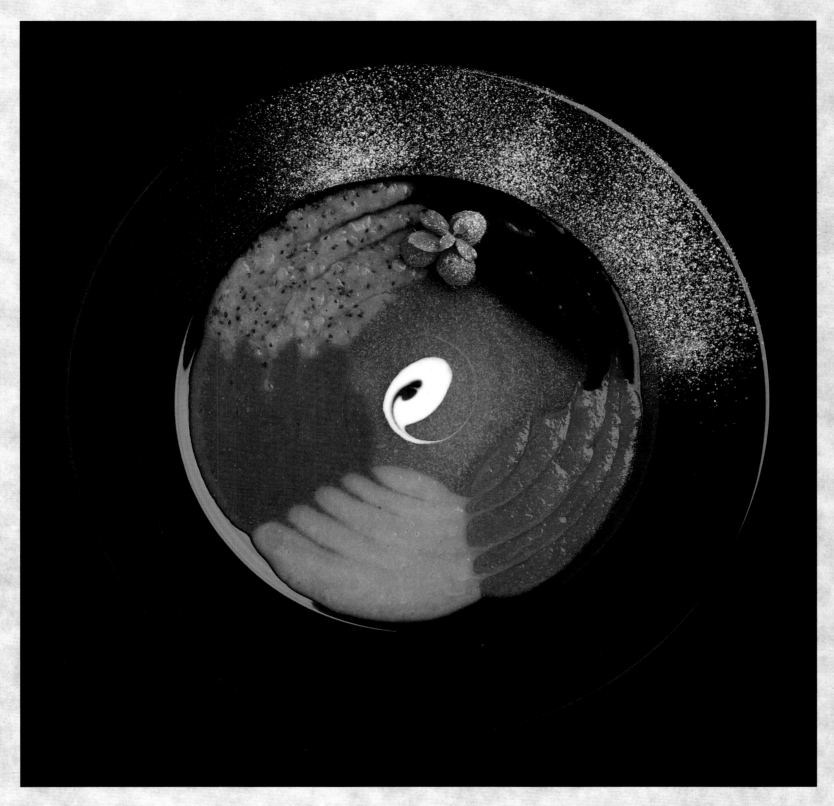

TO ENJOY this spectacular dish at its best, make it
according to the season, when you can enjoy the fruits in
their plumpest ripeness.

A culinary appreciation

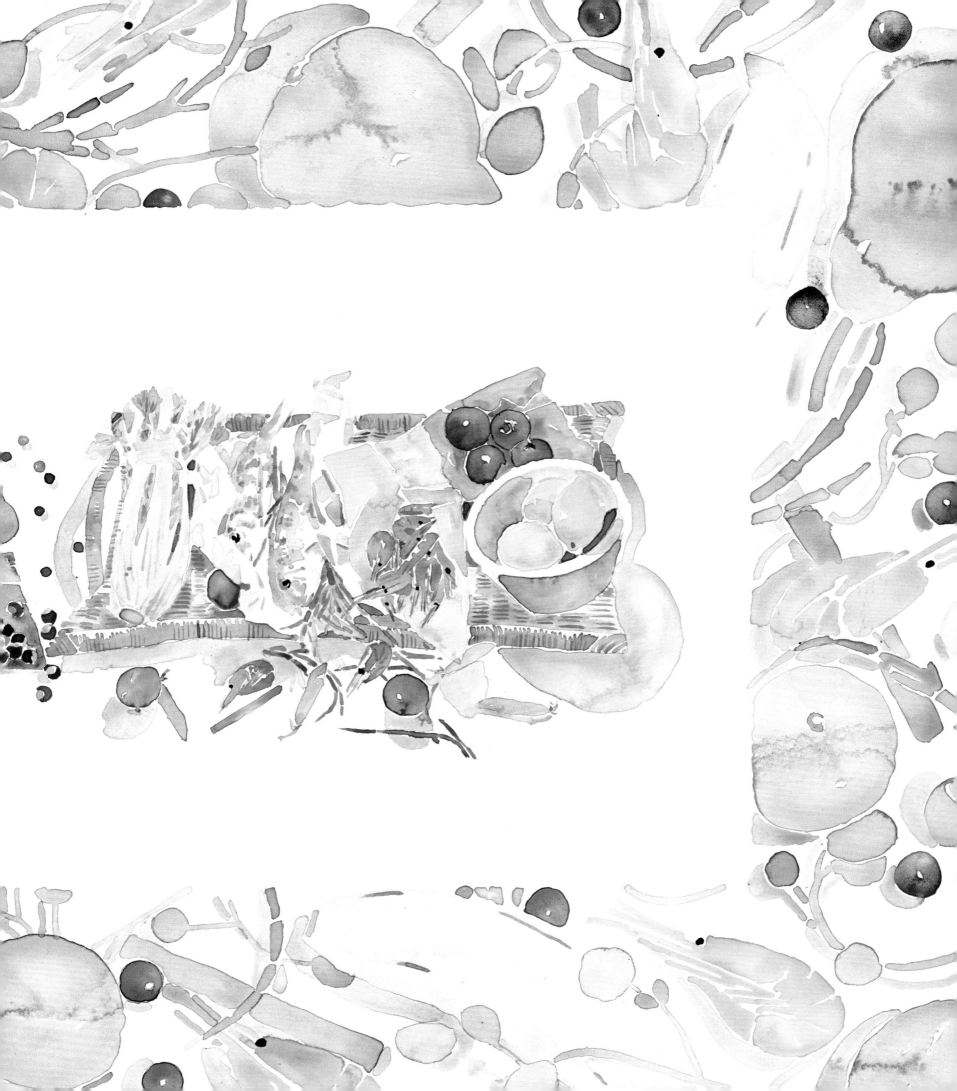

*M*ake a Fish Sauce (page 129), adding a teaspoon of fine, home-made Indian-style curry powder or paste to the shallots and continue in the normal way.

For each portion, take 100 g/4 oz of turbot fillet, carefully seasoned with salt and pepper, and poach it in fish stock for about 3 minutes. Remove, drain and place on a plate. Lay half a black truffle, cut into fine strips, and a sprig of Italian parsley on top of the turbot. A few delicate leaves of salad may be arranged in a small cluster on the plate. Spoon a little sauce on to the plate and serve the remainder separately.

ENOUGH FOR ONE

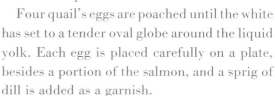

*T*his dish is quick to make. Prepare a marinade by combining the juice of two limes, 1 tablespoon each of cut chives and chopped dill, and $\frac{1}{2}$ teaspoon each of crushed coriander seeds and red peppercorns. The marinade is rubbed gently but firmly into a handsome 400 g/ 14 oz boned fillet of fresh wild Scottish salmon, then the fish is left in a cool place for 15 minutes.

The salmon fillet is sliced paper thin, and divided between four plates. A little of the remaining marinade is sprinkled over each portion together with a few dried violet petals.

Four quail's eggs are poached until the white has set to a tender oval globe around the liquid yolk. Each egg is placed carefully on a plate, besides a portion of the salmon, and a sprig of dill is added as a garnish.

ENOUGH FOR FOUR

page 44

page 45

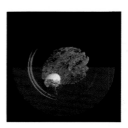

GRILLED MONKFISH
in warm vinaigrette with coriander

*M*ake the sauce by infusing a whole unpeeled garlic clove with almost a tablespoon of mature balsamic vinegar, eight crushed aromatic coriander seeds, some salt and crushed peppercorns, 3 tablespoons of the finest, virgin olive oil and 2 tablespoons of cold water.

Grill four little tails of monkfish, brushing them carefully with olive oil as they cook. Finely chop a sprig of tarragon and a couple of leaves of basil. Add these herbs to the sauce with 1 teaspoon of snipped chives and two tomatoes, which have been skinned, seeded and diced.

Pour the sauce on to four shallow plates, place the monkfish on top, and garnish with a sprig of basil.

ENOUGH FOR FOUR

SALMON TARTARE
with watercress sauce

*T*ake 50 g/2 oz of boned and skinned fillet of fine wild Scottish salmon. Cut it into small pieces but do not chop it. Marinate the salmon with the juice of half a lemon, a little salt, some freshly milled black pepper and a little finely cut dill. Leave for 10 minutes in a cool place.

Make a watercress sauce from 15 g/$\frac{1}{2}$ oz of watercress leaves, picked off their stalks. Blanch the leaves briefly, then refresh them in iced water and drain well. Purée the watercress leaves in a liquidiser with some yoghurt, seasoning, and a spoonful of double cream.

Pour the sauce on to a plate and set the salmon on top. Garnish at the side with three crisp salad leaves, a cherry tomato and a sprig of dill. Finally place a small spoonful of beluga caviar on the salmon tartar.

ENOUGH FOR ONE

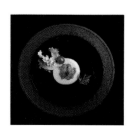

page 46

page 47

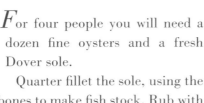

FILLET OF SOLE

in a parsley crust with steamed oysters

*F*or four people you will need a dozen fine oysters and a fresh Dover sole.

Quarter fillet the sole, using the bones to make fish stock. Rub with a cut lemon and season with salt and freshly milled pepper.

Cut the finest julienne from a slice of green and orange pepper, and daikon (long white radish).

Chop a shallot quite small, then soften it in 1 tablespoon of butter. Pour in 5 tablespoons of white wine and 200 ml/ 7 fluid oz of the fish stock and oyster liquor combined, and reduce. When reduced by half, add 150 ml/$\frac{1}{4}$ pint of double cream and simmer the sauce gently until thick and smooth. Season with salt, freshly milled pepper, lemon juice and 1 tablespoon of Sauternes.

Finely chop a small bunch of garden-fresh parsley. Fold over the ends of the sole fillets, top them with parsley and steam them until they are just opaque.

Steam the oysters in their half shells separately from the sole; sprinkle the julienne of vegetables over them and cook for just 5 seconds to keep the oysters moist and juicy.

Serve each oyster on a small pool of the sauce and place a fillet of sole in the centre.

ENOUGH FOR FOUR

page 47

CHARCOAL-GRILLED FILLET OF RED MULLET

with saffron noodles

*T*he noodles are made from a basic dough of 90 g/ 3½ oz of strong flour, sifted with 15 g/½ oz of fine wheat semolina and a pinch of salt. Steep a few saffron strands in 2 tablespoons of boiling water and strain the liquid. Mix the brilliant red saffron essence with half a beaten egg mixed with 1 teaspoon of olive oil. Then knead the liquid into the dry ingredients to form a very firm, smooth dough.

Allow the dough to rest in a cool place, covered with a damp cloth, for 2 to 3 hours, then divide it in half, and roll it out very thinly. Fold the sheets lengthwise, and then cut across into fine noodles.

Fillet a handsome red mullet, fresh from the Mediterranean, taking care to remove all the tiny bones. Cut each fillet in half, season with salt and freshly milled pepper, and smooth over some virgin olive oil from Lucca.

Boil the saffron noodles until al dente then sauté them in a shallow pan with melted butter, perfumed with a julienne of basil and a clove of garlic, and season with salt and pepper.

Grill the mullet over charcoal and fennel branches, basting with olive oil from time to time. Dress the noodles on two plates and lay the mullet over them. Garnish with two good sprigs of basil.

ENOUGH FOR TWO

page 48

KIPPER AND CREAM MOUSSELINE

with caviar

My mousseline is prepared from 150 g/5 oz each of sole or whiting and kipper fillets, all skinned and boned. Purée the fish finely, add a pinch of salt and stir in 2 tablespoons of double cream.

Strain the purée into a chilled basin, and set it over ice. Beat in 2 tablespoons of Noilly Prat and 200 ml/ 7 fluid oz of ice-cold double cream. Do this very-gradually, until the mousseline is shining and smooth. Season the mixture carefully with salt and pepper.

Butter a shallow rectangular dish and spread the mousseline into it. Poach the mousseline in a bain marie, in a moderate oven at 160°C/325°F/Gas 3 for about half an hour, or until set. Allow to cool then chill the mousseline thoroughly. Gently smooth a generous amount of caviar across the surface without breaking the fragile eggs.

The sauce is made from equal quantities of yoghurt and softly whipped cream, seasoned with salt, freshly milled pepper and a little fresh lemon juice.

Scoop the kipper mousseline from the dish with the tip of a hot spoon and lay it on beautiful plates. Dress each plate with a little sauce, a cherry tomato cut and filled with caviar and topped with a piece of chive, and a small bouquet of salad leaves.

Scatter over some cut chives and dice of celeriac to complete the garnish.

page 49

ENOUGH FOR FOUR

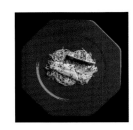

NEST OF COLOURED NOODLES

with sea bass

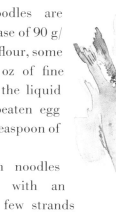

All the noodles are made with a base of 90 g/ 3½ oz of strong flour, some salt, 15 g/ ½ oz of fine semolina and the liquid from half a beaten egg mixed with 1 teaspoon of olive oil.

The saffron noodles are coloured with an infusion of a few strands of saffron in 2 tablespoons hot water; the spinach noodles take their colour from the addition of 25 g/1 oz of spinach purée, and the tomato noodles are coloured by 25 g/ 1 oz of tomato concasse.

Each portion of coloured dough is rested for 1 to 2 hours after kneading to make it silky smooth, and easy to roll out. The doughs are then cut into thin noodles and boiled until al dente.

Meanwhile, a little white wine sauce is made using dry white wine, fish stock and cream, then it is strained, seasoned and mixed with freshly chopped Italian parsley.

Bake two fine sea bass on a bed of fennel branches in a hot oven at 200°C/400°F/Gas 6 for 20 minutes. Fillet the fish carefully but do not remove the handsome silver skin.

Sauté the drained noodles in butter and arrange them on four plates. Lay the bass fillets on the noodles and pour just a little sauce over.

page 50

ENOUGH FOR FOUR

TWIN FILLETS OF RED MULLET

à la nage

*F*irst prepare a sound fish stock by washing about 500 g/1¼ lb of white fish bones and trimmings and making sure they are completely free of gills and roe. Finely cut 15 g/½ oz each of white mushroom and onion, and half that amount of celery. Tie a scrap of bay leaf, a small clove of garlic, a clove and a twist of lemon rind together with string. Place this bouquet garni in a clean pan with the fish bones, vegetables, 1.15 litres/2 pints of water and 3 tablespoons of white wine. Bring the water slowly to a simmer, removing the froth that rises to the surface, and cook very gently for 20 minutes. Strain carefully through muslin, and leave in a cool place to settle. Remove all the small eyes of fat that rise to the surface.

Ladle all the clear stock from the top and reduce it by half. Strain this again and allow it to cool.

Scale and fillet two red mullet with the utmost care as they contain many fine bones.

Place the red mullet trimmings in the base of a steamer and pour in the remaining stock. Take a slice of carrot and a leek leaf, and cut both into diamonds. Slice a button onion into fine rounds.

Now season and steam the fillets of red mullet for 2½ minutes. Strain the steaming stock and blanch the vegetables in it for a few seconds. Set the fish on two shallow, white plates, pour the reduced aromatic stock around, then garnish with the vegetables and add a few snipped chives.

page 51

ENOUGH FOR TWO

ROSETTE AND ROULADE OF SMOKED SALMON

with quark and chive mousse

*M*ake a mousse from 130 g/4½ oz quark. Whisk the drained quark with salt and freshly milled pepper, then fold in 2 tablespoons of finely cut chives. Soften 2 leaves of gelatine in cold water, squeeze the water from them and dissolve them in 2 tablespoons of warm water. Stir the dissolved gelatine into the quark. Whisk an egg white until stiff and fold it into the mousse.

Line four small glass dishes with eight thinly cut slices of smoked salmon and fill them with mousse. Divide the remaining mousse between four half slices of smoked salmon and roll up carefully into neat fingers. Chill in a cool place to set.

Now make a sauce, beginning by softening 1 tablespoon of finely chopped shallot in 1 tablespoon of butter. Pour 150 ml/¼ pint of dry white wine and 200 ml/7 fluid oz of fish stock over the softened shallot, then reduce by half. Add 450 ml/¾ pint of double cream and simmer gently until the sauce coats a spoon. Strain the sauce into two bowls. Liquidise one portion of the sauce with 2 tablespoons of finely cut fresh dill, basil and chives. Liquidise the remainder with ½ teaspoon of saffron strands soaked in 1 tablespoon of boiling water. Strain the sauces separately once more. Dress four pink plates with a spoonful of each of the sauces. Add a roulade and turned-out mousse to each plate. Garnish one of the mousses with chives and the other with dill.

page 52

ENOUGH FOR FOUR

GRILLED SCOTTISH SALMON

with ratatouille of Provençal vegetables

For each portion take 100 g/4 oz of middle cut salmon. Season the salmon on both sides with salt and freshly milled pepper, then grill it for about 2 minutes on each side.

The ratatouille is prepared from the ripest and brightest vegetables: green, yellow and red peppers, sweet scarlet tomatoes and a small aubergine cut in tiny dice. Altogether the vegetables should weigh 50 g/2 oz.

Now sauté a finely sliced shallot until soft in enough cold-pressed olive oil to cover the base of a small pan. Add the vegetables, 2 tablespoons of vegetable stock and season carefully. Cook the ratatouille gently until the vegetables are just tender.

When the ratatouille is ready and the salmon grilled, arrange some salad leaves on a beautiful plate. Add the salmon and the ratatouille, then garnish with a cherry tomato.

ENOUGH FOR ONE

CONSOMME OF FRESHWATER CRAYFISH

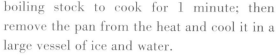

To begin the consommé, make 1.5 litres/2¾ pints of fine fish stock, of a clear, warm straw colour. Now take sixteen lively crayfish, and plunge them into the boiling stock to cook for 1 minute; then remove the pan from the heat and cool it in a large vessel of ice and water.

When cold remove all the tails from the crayfish, reserving the four most perfect ones for the final garnish of the consommé.

Roast the shells in a hot oven to concentrate their flavour. Chop the remaining tails and roasted shells and return them to the stock with a fine dice of a scant 25 g/ 1 oz each of tomato, carrot, leek and celery.

Whisk an egg white until frothy, and mix it into the cold stock, continuing to stir as it is brought very slowly to a simmer. Set on a very low heat to simmer, undisturbed, for about 30 minutes, until sparkling clear.

Strain the consommé slowly and carefully through a muslin-lined sieve and season it to perfection. Take a ladleful to heat the tails, and spoon the remaining hot liquid into four consommé cups.

Garnish each with a reserved crayfish tail and a carrot leaf.

ENOUGH FOR FOUR

page 53

page 54

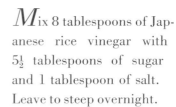

B LACK - BANDED BREAM

with wild garlic and lemon balm

*H*ere I have placed a cheery black-banded bream on a bed of wild garlic leaves, with a chilli and a sprig of lemon balm. Although the black-banded bream, with its bright fins and tail, is most striking, a red bream, golden-coloured gilt-head bream, or humble, grey sea bream can also be presented in this way. This fish is seasoned and rubbed with lemon juice, and it takes only 10 minutes to cook through in a hot oven at 200°C/400°F/Gas 6.

Open the parcel in front of your guest so that the mingled perfumes may be truly appreciated.

ENOUGH FOR ONE

S USHI

*M*ix 8 tablespoons of Japanese rice vinegar with 5½ tablespoons of sugar and 1 tablespoon of salt. Leave to steep overnight.

Wash 450 g/1 lb of sushi rice in a large bowl of cold water. Drain the rice for 30 minutes.

Put the rice in a heavy-bottomed saucepan. Add 850 ml/27 fluid oz cold water. Bring slowly to the boil. Increase the heat to high, cover and boil for 3 minutes. Reduce the heat to medium for 5 minutes. Reduce the heat to low; cook for 5 minutes.

Off the heat, place a piece of muslin under the lid and leave for 15 minutes.

Pour sushi dressing to taste over the hot rice. Use a rice paddle to mix the dressing and rice in a cutting motion. Fan the rice to cool it rapidly to body temperature. Mound it in a bowl. Cover with a damp cloth.

Sushi toppings may be raw or cooked. Seafood should be the finest and freshest. Peel eight large prawns. Take 175 g/6 oz each of fresh tuna, prepared and skinned squid, sea bream fillet and fresh salmon. Cut each portion of fish into eight, measuring $0.5 \times 4 \times 6$ cm/ $\frac{1}{4} \times 1\frac{1}{2} \times 2\frac{1}{2}$ inches. Add 2 tablespoons of rice vinegar to 250 ml/8 fluid oz of water to moisten your hands. Form about 1½ tablespoons of rice into a 5–6 cm/2–2½ inch long block. Spread a little wasabi (green horseradish mustard) on a piece of seafood. Press the rice on top. Shape the remaining sushi.

Simmer 250 ml/8 fluid oz of dark soy sauce with 5 teaspoons mirin (sweetened rice wine) for 2 to 3 minutes. Cool. Garnish the sushi with preserved, vinegared ginger and serve the dipping sauce separately.

MAKES ABOUT FORTY PIECES

page 54

page 55

STEAMED LOBSTER

with fresh herbs

*B*oil a small Scottish lobster in an aromatic broth of fish stock for 4 minutes, then cool it in the stock by standing the pan in a large vessel of iced water.

Finely chop half a bunch each of parsley, basil and dill. To this add the finely grated rind of a lemon, blanched and refreshed in cold water. Now make breadcrumbs from a slice of fresh bread, moisten them with a few drops of sunflower oil and stir in the herbs. Season with salt and freshly milled pepper.

When the lobster is cool, open the shell, and cut the tail meat into médaillons. Dip one end of each médaillon into the herb mixture. Make two bouquets of salad leaves with celery, chives, chervil, Italian parsley, watercress, and some mange tout which have been blanched in fish stock.

Present the lobster and salad on two pure white plates, each with a yellow tomato, and a light scattering of lobster roe.

ENOUGH FOR TWO

page 56

RENDEZ-VOUS DE FRUITS DE MER

*T*his dish is best warm, not hot, so that the delicate flavours and textures can be enjoyed to the full and at their most succulent.

From the fishmonger you will need four fine, fat scallops, 100 g/4 oz of prepared baby squid and a small cooked hen lobster. You will also need a small lettuce, four spring onions, a dozen small dried cloud ear mushrooms or wild mushrooms and 25 g/1 oz of tender, young runner beans.

Soak the cloud ear mushrooms for 20 minutes, before cooking them and adding to the rest of the ingredients.

Cook the mushrooms quickly in 15 g/$\frac{1}{2}$ oz butter, remove and set aside. Add 3 tablespoons of Noilly Prat, 5 tablespoons of white wine and double this amount of aromatic shellfish stock to the juices remaining in the pan. Reduce this by two-thirds, then whisk in 250 ml/ 8 fluid oz of double cream and simmer until the sauce coats a spoon. Season carefully with salt, freshly milled pepper and lemon juice.

Take the lobster from its shell and cut it into neat pieces. Slice the squid into rings and rinse the scallops in clean water. Season the shellfish and add it all to the sauce with the beans, cut in fine julienne, and the cloud ear mushrooms. Cook for 2 to 3 minutes.

Season the salad leaves and briefly steam them until they are barely warm but not limp. Then arrange them on four plates. Spoon the squid, scallops and lobster into the centre, and garnish with the spring onions.

page 57

ENOUGH FOR FOUR

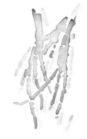

*F*irst make a court bouillon from 375 ml/13 fluid oz of water, 2 tablespoons of vinegar, 15 g/$\frac{1}{2}$ oz of the white part of a leek, sliced finely, and 25 g/1 oz each of carrot and onion. Simmer the bouillon for 30 minutes with a bouquet garni. Strain the bouillon through muslin, then reduce it by about one-third to intensify its flavour. Season with salt and freshly milled pepper.

You will need about six crayfish for each portion. Take a ladleful of boiling court bouillon to cook the crayfish – they should be barely submerged. Meanwhile blanch some samphire in boiling water for almost a minute.

While the crayfish are still warm, remove them from their shells and brush them with a little vinaigrette. If you like, reserve a couple of unpeeled crayfish to arrange on the plate. Arrange the crayfish on the drained samphire, displayed in beautiful sprays on an immaculate white plate.

ENOUGH FOR ONE

*A*ll the ingredients should be beautifully fresh and in perfect condition. Ground turmeric keeps its colouring properties, but it rapidly loses its aroma so it should be used as quickly as possible.

Make the sauce with 200 ml/7 fluid oz of shellfish-enriched fish stock, 50 ml/ 2 fluid oz of dry white wine, and 4 teaspoons of Noilly Prat. The combined liquids are reduced to 5 tablespoons with a finely chopped shallot. Add 175 ml/6 fluid oz of double cream, sprinkle with fresh turmeric and simmer gently until the sauce will coat a spoon. Season carefully and strain.

Take 100 g/4 oz each of fillet of sea bass, red mullet, salmon and turbot, and four scallops with plump coral roes. Season the seafood lightly with salt and freshly milled pepper.

Cut a small lightly cooked and shelled lobster into four pieces. Grill the fish, turning it carefully, so it browns evenly. Blanch a sliced button onion, a single leek leaf and a small new carrot.

Pour the brilliantly coloured sauce on to four plates, then divide the fish and seafood among them and scatter over the jewel-like vegetables.

ENOUGH FOR FOUR

STEAMED SCALLOPS

with a ratatouille of vegetables and sauce coraille

For two people you will need ten fresh scallops, taken from their shells and cleaned. Remove the corals and reserve them.

The ratatouille is made from one very large, ripe tomato, blanched and seeded, half each of a small red, orange and yellow pepper and two finely chopped shallots. The tomato and pepper are cut in fine dice. Reserve a tablespoon of the tomato.

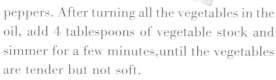

Heat 2 tablespoons of groundnut oil with three sprigs of thyme, four finely cut sprigs of basil and a clove of garlic, with its skin on. Add the shallots and soften them, then add the tomato and the peppers. After turning all the vegetables in the oil, add 4 tablespoons of vegetable stock and simmer for a few minutes, until the vegetables are tender but not soft.

For the sauce coraille poach the corals in Fish sauce for 5 minutes; liquidise and strain.

Season the scallops and steam them for 15 seconds. Remove the clove of garlic from the ratatouille and arrange the drained vegetables on two plates, in neat circles. Cut the scallops in half, and arrange them on top of the ratatouille. Chop the reserved tomato to a fine concasse and place it in the centre of the scallops with a sprig of basil for garnish. Pour the sauce around the scallops and ratatouille.

FISH SAUCE

Soften 1 tablespoon of finely chopped shallot in very little butter, then add 5 tablespoons of white wine and 10 tablespoons of fish stock and reduce by half.

page 59

Add 100 ml/4 fluid oz of double cream and simmer the sauce for a few moments. Strain the sauce through a fine sieve and season it carefully with salt and freshly milled pepper, and a few drops of lemon juice.

ENOUGH FOR TWO

A COCKTAIL OF SEAFOOD CONSOMME

For my consommé I use 1 litre/1¾ pints of cold, aromatic fish stock. To this I add 100 g/4 oz whiting fillet, skinned, boned and finely chopped, 50 g/ 2 oz of the finely sliced white part of

leek and an egg white beaten until frothy. A sprig of tarragon and a small ripe tomato give further flavour and the latter colours the consommé a warm amber. Bring the stock to a simmer in a clean pan rubbed with a lemon, stirring all the time, and add the roasted shell of a lobster.

When the stock comes to the boil, remove it from the heat, and leave to stand for an hour. Strain carefully and slowly through a muslin-lined sieve. Reduce the strained stock by one third to intensify its flavour; strain again and season.

For each person simmer half a small squid, which has been cleaned, trimmed and scored into petals with the point of a knife; a scampi; two mussels and a little lobster in 600 ml/1 pint of seasoned fish stock for a minute or so.

When cool, shell the scampi and the lobster. Arrange all the seafood in a beautiful cocktail glass with a scattering of lobster eggs.

Pour the sparkling clear soup over, and garnish with a perfect sprig of basil.

ENOUGH FOR ONE

page 61

SPICED CHICKEN LIVER PARFAIT

with tomato roses

It is important to clean the fresh chicken livers, before cutting them finely and weighing out 450 g/1 lb of them. Then liquidise them with 90 g/3½ oz of melted butter, 2½ tablespoons each of port and sherry, and five slices of truffle. Add the following spices to season the purée: freshly grated nutmeg, ground cloves, freshly milled white and black peppers and allspice, ground cinnamon, ginger and mace, pounded juniper berries and garlic, a scrap of bay leaf and a tiny sprig of fresh rosemary.

When all the ingredients are well mixed and fine, then sieve the purée. Prepare a terrine by lining it with strips of bacon stretched out thinly, then pour in the spiced livers, and fold over the ends of the bacon. Alternatively, the bacon can be omitted and the terrine lined with foil.

Now, place the terrine in a bain marie, cover and poach the parfait very slowly for 1 hour in a moderate oven at 160°C/325°F/Gas 3, until it is just firm when pressed.

Take the terrine from the bain marie, chill, and then unmould it. Remove the covering of bacon. Cut the spiced parfait with a sharp hot knife to show off its shining smoothness. Lay the slices of parfait on a plate prepared with a layer of set, clear chicken aspic. Garnish with three graceful stems of chives, rose flower shapes made of fine strips of tomato peel and chervil leaves.

page 66

ENOUGH FOR EIGHT

BREAST OF QUAIL HARLEQUIN

Cut the breast meat from four quails. Season the breasts well with salt and freshly milled pepper and sauté them carefully in 1 tablespoon of groundnut oil, allowing about 2 to 3 minutes cooking time on each side.

From the bones of the quail make an aromatic stock, similar to the one used for the Acqua d'oro (page 138). Reduce the stock slowly and carefully, skimming it as required until it is clear and syrupy, and thick enough to coat a spoon.

The yellow sauce is made by softening ½ tablespoon of chopped shallot in a few drops of groundnut oil. Then 3 tablespoons of white wine and 5 tablespoons of quail or poultry stock are added and reduced until only 4 tablespoons remain. When you reach this stage, add 4 tablespoons of double cream and enough turmeric to colour the sauce, and simmer gently. The sauce is ready when it is thick enough to coat a spoon.

Poach four fresh quail's eggs and arrange them on a spoonful of sauce on the chosen plates. Make four small clusters of salad leaves, including some frisée, chives, chervil, parsley and radicchio (or use whatever salad ingredients are fresh and colourful at the market) and arrange them at the side of the plates. Glaze the quail breasts with the reduced, syrupy stock and arrange two on each plate.

page 67

ENOUGH FOR FOUR

WARM CHICKEN

with Japanese salad

*Y*ou will need a 100 g/4 oz plump and succulent breast of maize-fed chicken. Season the chicken and sauté it very slowly in a little sunflower oil for 3 to 4 minutes on both sides, until it is cooked.

While still warm, slice the chicken thinly, and serve it with crisp batons of celery and carrot, and a radish flower. Turn a few leaves of lamb's lettuce and radicchio in a sherry vinegar and olive oil vinaigrette, then arrange them attractively at the side.

ENOUGH FOR ONE

page 69

BREAST OF CHICKEN

on broccoli cream sauce with julienne vegetables

*N*eatly trim four perfect breasts of maize-fed chicken, remove their skin and carefully season them with salt and freshly milled pepper.

Cut a courgette, two sticks of celery and a carrot into fine julienne.

The sauce is made from white wine and cream, flavoured with an aromatic chicken stock. Then, when this is finally reduced to the correct consistency, 50 to 75 g/2 to 3 oz of cooked broccoli is added. Only the greenest and most tender tips of the broccoli florets are added, then they are puréed with the white wine sauce. The sauce is carefully seasoned and strained.

Steam the chicken breasts for 5 to 6 minutes. Blanch the vegetable julienne. Pour the broccoli sauce on to four superb black plates, and pipe onto it four dark, translucent circles of melted glace de volaille (a chicken glaze produced by greatly reducing an excellent stock). Draw the glace de volaille to the centre with the point of a knife, then lay the chicken breast in the sauce. Place the hot julienne on top, and garnish each portion with a sprig of tarragon.

ENOUGH FOR FOUR

page 69

STEAMED BABY CHICKEN
on pine needles

*T*o give flavour to the delicate flesh, cream 25 g/1 oz soft butter with salt, freshly milled pepper and 2 tablespoons of chopped herbs, such as tarragon, chives or parsley.

Separate skin from the flesh covering the breast of a plump poussin and smooth the herb butter under the skin. Blanch some tender young vegetables in boiling vegetable stock, and refresh them in ice-cold water.

Season the poussin, and make a small cradle from foil large enough to hold the poussin and vegetables. Steam the poussin over a bed of pine needles in a bamboo steamer for 35 minutes, adding the vegetables 3 minutes before the end of the cooking time. Serve straight from the bamboo steamer.

ENOUGH FOR ONE

page 71

POACHED QUAIL IN ITS BROTH
with baby vegetables

*T*he stock is made from 450 g/1 lb quail bones and trimmings, from which you have removed the breasts, and an equal amount of veal bones. Both are carefully browned all over in a little sunflower oil. They are transferred to a clean pan, and covered with almost 1.75 litres/3 pints of water, and a pinch of sea salt is added, then the stock is simmered for three quarters of an hour. The stock should be skimmed during cooking. Then an unpeeled shallot is browned directly on the hot plate and added to the stock with the trimmings from eight new carrots, two leeks and four baby turnips.

A celery leaf, a sprig of thyme and a few stalks of parsley are tied into a bouquet garni and placed in the stock to give it a round and sweet flavour as it is brought once again to the simmer and carefully skimmed. After 30 minutes the stock is strained and cooled.

To make the stock sparkling clear, 200 g/7 oz of quail and lean poultry flesh are minced together and mixed with two egg whites, 40 g/1½ oz each of tomato and celery and a few tarragon leaves. This is thoroughly mixed with the cold stock and 150 ml/¼ pint of dry white wine. The stock should be stirred as it is brought to a simmer, then it is left over low heat to bubble quietly, undisturbed, for 30 minutes. Slowly and carefully, strain the stock through a muslin-lined sieve.

Season the stock. Transfer several ladles of it to a clean pan. Boil four little cauliflowers, four kohlrabi, a dozen baby carrots, two leeks, cut into eight, some potatoes, four turnips, and a handful of broad beans until al dente. Remove the vegetables. Blanch four Savoy cabbage leaves in the stock.

Lightly sauté eight seasoned quail breasts until tender and golden. Place on the vegetables, on four soup plates. Pour over the boiling quail stock, and garnish with thyme.

ENOUGH FOR FOUR

page 72

MOUSSELINE OF CHICKEN LIVER

with raspberry coulis

*P*repare the finest chicken liver mousseline possible, from 225 g/8 oz of fresh chicken livers, two shallots, 100 g/4 oz of unsalted butter and a pinch each of mixed spice and allspice.

Clean the livers, and chop the shallots finely. Cook everything together for 5 to 6 minutes, then let the mixture cool slightly, and purée it very finely in a liquidiser. Press the purée through a fine sieve and leave it to cool, closely covered.

Whip 4 tablespoons double cream, and lightly fold it into the chicken liver purée. Season with salt and freshly milled pepper, then transfer to a glass dish and chill until firm.

With a hot spoon, scoop out two nice coquilles, or quenelle shapes, of the chicken liver mousseline. Serve with a coulis of raspberries, made in a liquidiser using 100 g/4 oz of fresh raspberries with a little lemon juice and icing sugar to taste. Garnish each portion with a fresh raspberry, mint, and a few salad leaves.

ENOUGH FOR FOUR

POACHED FILLET OF BEEF

with horseradish vinaigrette

*T*o poach the beef you will need about 600 ml/1 pint of rich brown stock, salt and freshly milled pepper.

The sauce requires a large sweet tomato, skinned, seeded and cut into dice. In a small bowl mix together 1 teaspoon of sherry vinegar with 2 tablespoons of olive oil and 1 teaspoon of grated horseradish. Season the mixture with salt and freshly milled pepper, then stir in the prepared tomato.

Heat the beef stock to simmering point. Carefully season a 150 g/5 oz trimmed médaillon from the head of a fillet of beef and poach it in the stock for about 5 minutes.

When the médaillon of beef is cooked, remove it and drain, then set it on a lovely plate. Pour over the horseradish vinaigrette and cover with the cloche to keep warm. The vinaigrette will act as a marinade for the fillet, and add to its succulence and taste, as it is being served.

ENOUGH FOR ONE

page 73

page 74

HORS D'OEUVRE OF SALMON CAVIAR
and elixir of beef

I make beef consommé with the sweet bones from the loin, making sure they are evenly coloured in a hot oven, and browning the aromatic vegetables separately, so there is no risk of charring them.

When the stock made from the browned bones and vegetables is completed, cooled, and all the fat removed, 1.15 litres/2 pints of the cooled stock are clarified with 150 g/5 oz of minced lean beef and its flavour is mellowed by adding 15 g/½ oz of leek, and just a little less of carrot and celery. Two frothy egg whites are whisked in with the beef and the mirepoix of leek, carrot and celery. All are brought slowly to the boil. When the egg whites cluster, the consommé is allowed to bubble undisturbed over low heat for about 30 minutes, increasing in flavour while becoming sparkling clear.

When it has been strained slowly through scalded muslin, the consommé is ready for its final garnish. Ladle a little into a saucepan. Add sixteen soaked black fungus or cloud ear mushrooms, one or two finely sliced spring onions and a little fresh green ginger, finely sliced, as the Chinese would say, into silken threads. Lastly, add four fine slices of well-hung fillet of beef.

Ladle the remaining consommé into four bowls and divide the prepared ingredients between them. Lastly, to each portion, add the crowning garnish of salmon caviar, served in a tiny bowl.

ENOUGH FOR FOUR

page 75

SWEETBREAD SOLO
with tomato coulis

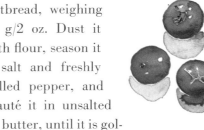

*T*ake a piece of prepared veal sweetbread, weighing about 50 g/2 oz. Dust it lightly with flour, season it with salt and freshly milled pepper, and sauté it in unsalted butter, until it is golden brown.

Make a smooth coulis from two very ripe, deeply coloured tomatoes – do this by liquidising the tomatoes finely and cooking the purée with a little lemon juice, some salt and freshly milled pepper.

Strain the coulis when it is cooked and add a pinch of sugar.

Serve the veal sweetbread on the tomato coulis. For garnish add a spring onion which has been trimmed and finely snipped into strips, then left in iced water to curl. Add a cherry tomato and scatter some chives over to complete the garnish.

ENOUGH FOR ONE

page 76

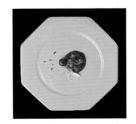

134

ROAST RACK OF LAMB

with wild mushrooms and roasted shallots

*T*his is a rustic, country dish which I love to cook from time to time. It takes me back to my early days on the farm, to times when I returned famished from a day's hay-making to find the kitchen filled with the heady aroma of roasted lamb and onions.

A tender rack of South Downs' lamb is trimmed until only a nut of meat remains attached to the cutlet bones. The fat around the kidney is shaved away to form an even coating. Then the joint is seasoned and roasted to pink perfection.

Eight trompettes de morte (horn of plenty mushrooms) are sautéed in butter, then two tight little heads of Savoy cabbage are blanched and added to the pan. These vegetables are sautéed together until they shine in the pan of foaming butter.

The lamb is served on the vegetables, glazed with a glossy brown sauce made from lamb stock and served with shallots that are roasted in their skins. A sprig of rosemary is the final, aromatic garnish.

ENOUGH FOR SIX

page 77

CARPACCIO

with a ruffle of cheese

I like to use a fresh beef fillet (about 50–75 g/ 2–3 oz), chilled until firm in the freezer before cutting it into fine slices. These are flattened further by the careful use of a rolling pin. They are then laid on a plate, and brushed generously with a dressing made from 2 tablespoons strong beef consommé and 2 teaspoons of olive oil, seasoned with salt and freshly milled pepper and containing $\frac{1}{2}$ teaspoon of mixed finely chopped chervil, parsley and chives.

A frill of Swiss cheese (Tête de Moine) and bitterish lollo rosso leaves are placed in the centre.

ENOUGH FOR ONE

page 78

WELSH MOUNTAIN LAMB
with truffle and herb crust

To cook potatoes so that they look like the petals of a flower, you need to slice them very thinly, then arrange them on a buttered baking sheet in an even circle. Brush them with melted butter, season with salt and freshly milled pepper, and bake in a hot oven at 200°C/400°F/Gas 6 until golden and tender.

Finely chop some tarragon and parsley, then mix these herbs with a teaspoon of truffle juice.

Fry a noisette of lamb, taken from a small saddle of Welsh mountain lamb, for 2 to 3 minutes on each side in a teaspoon of oil, until it is pink and tender within, and caramelised to a golden crust on the surface.

Slide the cooked potatoes on to a beautiful plate and place the noisettes in the centre. Spoon the herbs and truffle juices over the lamb.

ENOUGH FOR ONE

page 79

GULL'S EGG SERVED ON A WATERCRESS SAUCE
with salmon caviar

For the sauce use 25 g/1 oz of watercress leaves, refreshed and drained, and puréed in a liquidiser with 5 tablespoons of double cream. Bring the sauce to the boil, then strain it and season it carefully with salt and freshly milled pepper.

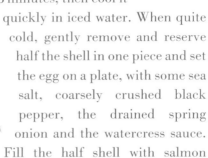

Meanwhile trim a spring onion and snip the green end into fine strips then place it in iced water to open the leaves.

Boil a gull's egg for 8 minutes, then cool it quickly in iced water. When quite cold, gently remove and reserve half the shell in one piece and set the egg on a plate, with some sea salt, coarsely crushed black pepper, the drained spring onion and the watercress sauce.

Fill the half shell with salmon caviar and arrange it on the plate.

ENOUGH FOR ONE

page 80

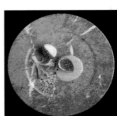

LEEK TERRINE
with trompettes de morte

*T*rim 1 kg/2 lb of leeks and cut them to fit a mould. Tie them in equal bundles, and cook them in boiling salted water until tender. Refresh the leeks in ice-cold water, then ensure that they are well drained.

Lightly cook about 225 g/8 oz of fresh trompettes de morte (or horn of plenty mushrooms) in a little oil.

First the terrine is lined carefully with cling film. Set aside a quarter of the trompettes de morte for the sauce. Press half the remaining mushrooms into the terrine. Half the leeks are gently smoothed into the terrine and pressed close together, the green and white ends alternating with each other. The remaining mushrooms are pressed on top of the leeks, then the rest of the leeks are layered in the terrine. When filled completely, the terrine is covered and the leeks are pressed, then it is kept in a cold place for at least 6 hours.

The sauce, is made from a light mayonnaise. Make it from an egg, 450 ml/ $\frac{3}{4}$ pint of sunflower oil and 300 ml/$\frac{1}{2}$ pint of hazelnut oil with a few drops of light wine vinegar or sherry vinegar. Season the mayonnaise with salt and freshly milled pepper and liquidise it with two-thirds of the reserved trompettes de morte. The sauce should be the colour of stone. To make a deeply coloured mushroom sauce, place a few tablespoons of the sauce in a small liquidiser and blend it with the remaining mushrooms, then strain both sauces separately. The sauces should be the consistency of double cream.

To serve, pour a little sauce on the plate, and lay a slice of leek terrine on top. Circle with some dots of the darker sauce, and form them into a light-hearted border, by drawing the tip of a knife through the dots.

page 81

ENOUGH FOR TWELVE

SCRAMBLED EGGS
with caviars

*Y*ou will need to cut the tops off the eggs and empty them into a bowl. Rinse the shells clean, then drain them well. Scramble three eggs in the normal way, by stirring them over hot water with a scrap of fine butter, a little cream, salt and freshly milled pepper.

Set the shells in crystal, china or porcelain holders and pour the scrambled eggs inside. Cover with a generous spoonful each of royal beluga, salmon eggs and lobster eggs.

ENOUGH FOR THREE

page 83

*F*or the basic stock, brown 400 g/14 oz of quail bones and trimmings, and a small knuckle of veal all over in 1 tablespoon of hot groundnut oil.

Then drain them and place them in a pan. Cover with 1.4 litres/2½ pints of cold water and a pinch of salt and simmer for 45 minutes. To create exactly the right flavour brown half an unpeeled shallot directly on the hot plate and add it to the stock together with 25 g/1 oz each of trimmed leek, celery and carrot.

The quail stock must be simmered for a further 30 minutes to extract the fullest flavour from the ingredients, then it can be strained through muslin and cooled.

Clarify the stock to make a crystal consommé. Mince 200 g/7 oz each of quail flesh and lean poultry flesh together. Mix with two egg whites, 50 g/2 oz each of diced tomato and celery, a few parsley stalks and tarragon leaves. Stir into the stock. Stir in 150 ml/¼ pint dry white wine.

The combination of poultry and quail meats accentuate the flavour of the quail stock and the consommé will be slightly sweetened by the vegetables and flavoured by the herbs.

Keep stirring over a medium heat as the soup comes to the boil, then allow it to simmer undisturbed for 20 minutes. Season with salt and freshly milled pepper.

When the consommé is sparkling clear, the clusters of egg white should be carefully skimmed from the surface. This done, ladle the consommé through a muslin-lined sieve into a clean pan and reheat it gently.

Boil four quail's eggs for 2 minutes, until firm enough to peel but soft within. Wrap them in a little gold leaf. Serve the eggs in the hot consommé in fine porcelain consommé cups, garnished with fragments of gold leaf.

ENOUGH FOR FOUR

page 83

au citron vert

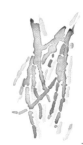

*T*he seven cherry tomatoes are first poached in 300 ml/½ pint of clear vegetable stock for a few moments, then drained and their skins removed. The poaching liquor is seasoned with the juice of half a lime, a pinch of sugar, 1 teaspoon of clear soy sauce and some freshly milled pepper. The finely grated rind of a perfect, fragrant lime is added to the sauce.

Just 25 g/1 oz of samphire is blanched in plenty of boiling salted water, then drained well and arranged on a beautiful plate. The tomatoes are arranged attractively on the samphire and dressed with the sauce.

ENOUGH FOR ONE OR TWO

page 84

TIMBALE OF THREE VEGETABLE MOUSSES

Prepare enough carrots, turnips and broccoli florets to yield 50 g/2 oz of each when trimmed and cooked, puréed and strained.

For each vegetable, soften 1 leaf of gelatine in cold water, then dissolve them separately, each in 2 tablespoons of warm water. Mix each vegetable purée separately with 25 ml/1 fluid oz of cream or quark and a portion of dissolved gelatine, then season to taste with salt and freshly milled pepper. Add a little mace to the turnip purée and cinnamon to the carrot purée.

Whisk an egg white until stiff and fold it into the carrot purée, then pour it into the base of a glass dish. Place in the freezer to set quickly. When the carrot layer is firm, whisk another egg white and fold it into the turnip mixture, then set it as before. Repeat with the broccoli mousse.

Make an aspic jelly from 300 ml/$\frac{1}{2}$ pint of clarified chicken stock, using $3\frac{1}{2}$ leaves of gelatine. Cut a small red and green pepper into neat dice, then sprinkle both over the three mousses and pour the aspic jelly over. Leave in a cool place to set.

Use a hot spoon to remove each portion and serve on a black plate, which will highlight the tenderness of the mousse and the soft colours of vegetables. Serve a spoonful of seasoned quark, with each portion. Dust with paprika and garnish with chives.

page 85

ENOUGH FOR SIX

RENDEZ-VOUS DE POMMES D'AMOUR

Blanch six fine, sweet tomatoes, and remove their skins. Discard the seeds and liquid, then cut the tomatoes into quarters and drain the transluscent flesh.

The basic tomato mousse is made from 225 g/8 oz of ripe, sweet tomato concasse, 1 teaspoon of tomato purée, a pinch of sugar, 2 leaves of gelatine and 175 to 250 ml/ 6 to 8 fluid oz of seasoned whipped cream.

Soften the gelatine in cold water. When the tomato concasse is cooked to a thick purée, add the lightly sweetened tomato purée, then liquidise the mixture to a fine texture and sieve it. Drain the gelatine and dissolve it in the hot tomato mixture. Season with salt and freshly milled pepper, then allow to cool until just beginning to set and fold in the seasoned whipped cream.

Fill a shallow china or glass dish with most of the tomato mousse, and leave it to set in a cold place. Smooth the remainder into a rounded terrine, following the curved sides, and layering in the tomato quarters. Season between the layers with salt and freshly milled pepper. Chill to set.

Meanwhile, marinate six brilliant-yellow tomatoes in a vinaigrette, then drain them.

Cut the terrine into six slices. Using a hot spoon, scoop out six rounded ovals (coquilles) from the dish of tomato mousse and arrange both on six plates.

Place a spoon of soured cream on each plate and place the yellow tomatoes on top. Garnish the coquilles with a few delicate sprigs of mustard and cress.

page 87

ENOUGH FOR SIX

*B*lanch 50 g/2 oz perfect spinach leaves, refresh them and drain them thoroughly, squeezing as much of the water as possible from the leaves.

Line a small buttered mould with the largest leaves, then place the rest in a liquidiser with an egg and 5 tablespoons of double cream, salt, freshly milled pepper and freshly grated nutmeg. Blend the ingredients for a few seconds, then pour the purée into the spinach-lined mould. Place the mould in a bain marie, and cook gently in a moderate oven at 160°C/325°F/Gas 3 for about 25 to 30 minutes, until set but soft in the centre.

Meanwhile make a lovely saffron sauce, using a vegetable stock as the base. Soften a chopped shallot in 1 tablespoon of butter, then add 5 tablespoons of dry white wine and almost 300 ml/½ pint of vegetable stock. Reduce by half, then pour in 150 ml/¼ pint of double cream or whipping cream.

Simmer the sauce slowly and season it carefully. Infuse a few strands of saffron in 1 tablespoon of boiling water for 10 minutes. When the sauce is thick, smooth and creamy stir in the saffron and season with salt and freshly milled pepper.

Unmould the timbale, pour the saffron sauce around it and serve with a little new carrot as a garnish. Introduce fine wisps of infused saffron water to fleck the sauce and complete the garnish.

page 88

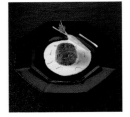

ENOUGH FOR ONE

*T*he ravioli are made from 100 g/4 oz of strong flour, ¼ teaspoon of salt, 1 teaspoon of oil, an egg and slightly less than 1 tablespoon of water. These ingredients are kneaded together to make a smooth dough, then covered and left to rest in a cool place.

The basic chicken consommé requires 1.15 litres/2 pints of rich, golden chicken stock, to which I add 50 g/2 oz of lean minced chicken, a roasted chicken carcase or some lean browned trimmings, 1 egg white, 40 g/1½ oz chopped leek and scant 25 g/1 oz each of celery and carrots, also cut into small pieces. Stir all the ingredients together well, then set them aside for an hour in a cold place.

Then bring the stock with all its flavourings to a simmer in a clean pan, rubbed with a cut lemon, stirring occasionally.

When the stock comes to the boil, draw the pan to the side of the heat; allow the stock to cook gently, undisturbed, for 30 minutes. The egg white will separate into clouds, and the consommé will bubble through, sparkling clear. Season with salt and pepper, and add a tablespoon or so of truffle essence in the very last stages of cooking. Filter the consommé carefully through a sieve lined with scalded muslin.

Cut the ravioli dough in half, and roll it out very thinly using a dusting of flour if necessary. Cut into a dozen squares, and fold them into bishop's hat shapes or mitres. Bring a large ladleful of the consommé to the boil and cook the ravioli until tender, but al dente, then drain them.

Heat the remaining consommé until it is piping hot. Slip sliced truffles into the ravioli and divide them between four beautiful soup plates. Ladle in the sparkling consommé and garnish with delicate herb sprigs.

page 89

ENOUGH FOR FOUR

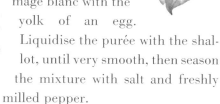

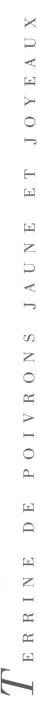

*T*o make the filling cut half a shallot into fine dice and soften them in a teaspoon of butter. Purée 150 g/5 oz of cooked young turnip and strain it. Take 5 tablespoons of the turnip purée and stir in 2½ tablespoons of fromage blanc with the yolk of an egg.

Liquidise the purée with the shallot, until very smooth, then season the mixture with salt and freshly milled pepper.

Cut some tiny vegetable dice from two slices each of red pepper, carrot and turnip. Blanch the vegetable dice for a few seconds in boiling salted water, drain and fold half of them into the mousse.

The ivory-coloured sauce is made from a teaspoon of shallot which is softened in butter, 2 tablespoons of dry white wine and double the quantity of vegetable stock. The liquid is reduced by half, then 50 ml/2 fluid oz of double cream are added and the sauce is simmered gently. When thick enough to coat a spoon, the sauce is strained and seasoned.

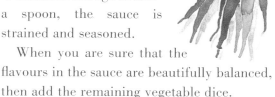

When you are sure that the flavours in the sauce are beautifully balanced, then add the remaining vegetable dice.

Trim away the ends from eight mange tout and pipe the filling into them. Steam the stuffed mange tout for 3 minutes then brush them with a little vinaigrette and cut them on the diagonal. Serve with the sauce and scatter a little diced red pepper over to garnish.

page 90

ENOUGH FOR FOUR

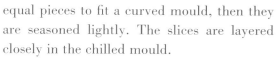

*T*he terrine is made from two large red or yellow peppers which are roasted in the oven, or under the grill, until just charred. Then the skin is easily removed and the peppers are cut in half to be trimmed of the core and seeds. The peppers must be cut into equal pieces to fit a curved mould, then they are seasoned lightly. The slices are layered closely in the chilled mould.

A clear pepper or vegetable aspic is prepared and softened gelatine is dissolved in it. This is gently poured into the pepper terrine to set the slices softly in place. Keep it in a cool place until set.

The sauce is made from the pepper trimmings, and one extra pepper, a small, finely chopped shallot, a large clove of fresh sweet garlic and a sprig of thyme. The ingredients are simmered with 200 ml/7 fluid oz of vegetable or chicken stock for 15 minutes, during which time the pan is kept covered. The sauce is liquidised, and seasoned with salt and pepper. Then it is returned to the heat and cooked gently until it is smooth and creamy.

After straining, the sauce is cooled and poured on to a handsome plate. A slice of the terrine is laid in the centre.

ENOUGH FOR FOUR

page 91

*T*ake 75 g/3 oz of raw chicken breast and purée it with a pinch of salt and 1 tablespoon of double cream. Pass the purée through a sieve, then set it to chill. Infuse a few saffron strands in 1 tablespoon of boiling water for 10 minutes; strain and cool. Add the saffron liquid to 150 ml/¼ pint of cold double cream. Over ice, beat the saffron cream into the chicken purée, then season the mixture carefully with salt, freshly milled pepper and ground mace.

Liquidise 100 g/4 oz cooked carrots to a fine purée, with about 2 tablespoons of double cream to make the mixture swirl in the liquidiser like double cream. Strain the purée and whisk in one small egg. Season with salt, freshly milled pepper and cinnamon.

Place the carrot purée and the saffron mousseline in separate piping bags fitted with plain nozzles. Pipe a border of carrot purée around the sides of two buttered moulds, then immediately pipe the saffron mousseline into the centre. Gently tap the moulds on the table to remove any air bubbles but take care not to mix the two mixtures. Place both moulds in a bain marie, and poach the mousseline in a moderate oven at 160°C/325°F/Gas 3 for about 25 minutes, until set.

Cut little diamonds from half a small red and yellow pepper and toss them with some salad leaves.

Unmould the timbales on to two lustrous plates, which show clearly the brilliance of their colours, and garnish them with the salad and a fresh basil leaf.

page 92

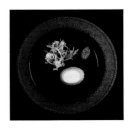

ENOUGH FOR TWO

*B*lanch 100–175 g/4–6 oz of vegetables per person in salted water and, while still warm, place them in a hot marinade of 300 ml/½ pint of water, 75 ml/3 fluid oz of cold-pressed olive oil, the juice of a lemon, and plentiful seasoning of salt, whole peppercorns and coriander seeds.

After 3 to 4 hours, remove the vegetables from the marinade and arrange them on a plate, allowing their shapes and colours to create a natural beauty which so pleases the eye and excites the appetite.

In the photograph of a single portion on page 93, shining in the marinade you will find a baby Savoy cabbage, cauliflower, kohlrabi, tiny turnips, carrots, leeks, corn, fennel and a chilli. They are all sprinkled with finely cut chives.

page 93

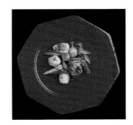

ENOUGH FOR FOUR

You will need to cut half each of a red pepper and yellow pepper into small, fine strips. Similarly, cut up the head of a floret of Cape broccoli, and a quarter of a small head of cauliflower. Cut 50 g/2 oz of French beans and 50 g/2 oz of young carrots into julienne.

Blanch all the vegetables separately in a vegetable stock and cool the pan in iced water. Cook a very small celeriac, cut into pieces, in milk until quite soft, then drain and purée it until very smooth. You will need 300 g/10 oz of celeriac purée.

Strain the purée and liquidise it with 2 tablespoons of cream, salt and freshly milled pepper, two eggs and one egg yolk. Gently stir in the drained vegetables. Using a piping bag, fill a soaked and drained sausage skin with the mixture, and twist it into individual sausages.

For the smooth green sauce, cook 100 g/4 oz of shelled broad beans in vegetable stock until tender. Then purée and season them with salt and freshly milled pepper. Liquidise the purée to a subdued foam with a little cream until it is of a coating consistency.

Brush the sausages with a little sunflower oil, and place under a hot grill for 4 minutes on each side before setting on to the sauce.

ENOUGH FOR SIX TO EIGHT

page 94

Take two small new potatoes, if possible just dug from the earth. Wrap them in foil and bake at 200°C/400°F/Gas 6 for 15 to 20 minutes, or until they are tender. When the potatoes are cool enough to handle, take the foil off them, then wrap one potato in silver leaf and the other in gold leaf.

Make a deep lengthways incision along the potatoes and use a little pressure to open the potatoes slightly. Fill with soured cream with some finely cut chives, seasoned with a little salt and freshly milled pepper.

Crown each potato with a generous serving of royal beluga caviar and set them on a plate.

ENOUGH FOR ONE

page 95

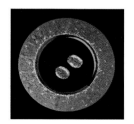

MANGO ON BLACKBERRY VELVET

*C*ut two generous slices off a large mango. Score the flesh with the point of a sharp knife without cutting through the skin of the fruit.

Make a blackberry sauce by liquidising 100 g/ 4 oz of blackberries with a little lemon juice and icing sugar. Strain the sauce. Peel and purée the remaining mango, then pass it through a sieve.

Pour the blackberry sauce on to two plates. Curve the skin of the mango slices so that the scored fruit stands proud as you set them on the sauce. Pour a little mango purée on to the blackberry sauce, and marble it with the back of a spoon. Decorate with two fresh violets or wild pansies and mint leaves.

ENOUGH FOR TWO

page 98

POACHED PEAR

served with crème à l'Anglaise of caramel and chocolate

*T*ake two fine pears, ripened in the late autumn sun, peel them, remove their cores and poach them in a sugar syrup containing the rind and juice of an orange. Leave the pears to cool in the syrup.

Make four little biscuit cups from the batter used to make Almond tuile biscuits (page 151). Leave them to cool.

Make a crème à l'Anglaise with five egg yolks, 75 g/3 oz of vanilla sugar and 600 ml/1 pint of creamy milk, cooked in a double boiler with a vanilla pod opened into the sauce. When the sauce coats the back of a spoon, remove the basin from over the hot water. Set aside 450 ml/¾ pint sauce and halve the rest.

Make a caramel from 50 g/2 oz of sugar and 2 tablespoons of water, boiling it to a dark, tea colour. Off the heat, carefully add 150 ml/¼ pint of double cream. Add the caramel cream to one small bowl of vanilla sauce.

To the other small bowl of sauce, add 50 g/ 2 oz of melted bitter Swiss chocolate. Stir until smooth. Allow all sauces to cool.

Blanch 25 g/1 oz of fine Persian pistachios in milk to remove their skins. Chop them but not too finely.

Stir 150 ml/¼ pint of double cream into the vanilla crème à l'Anglaise and pour some into four large plates. Set a pear half in the middle of each.

Following the curved outlines of the plates, add lines of the chocolate and caramel sauces, then marble them. Spoon pistachio ice cream into the pears. Fill the biscuit cups with raspberries and mint, and add to the plates. Add chocolate sauce to represent pear stalks. Sprinkle pistachio fragments in the sauce.

ENOUGH FOR FOUR

page 99

Remove the crusts from between six and eight slices of good white bread and use them to line a 900 ml/1½ pint pudding basin. Hull and pick over 450 g/1 lb of blackberries, black and red currants, raspberries and a few strawberries – all must be in perfect condition and glowing with freshness. Soften 3 leaves of gelatine in cold water.

Place the fruit in a pan, add 100 ml/4 fluid oz of water, 100 g/4 oz of sugar and the juice of a lemon. Bring to a simmer then add the drained gelatine and allow the leaves to steep in the liquid, off the heat, until completely dissolved.

Arrange a layer of fruit in the base of the basin and spoon over a little of the garnet-coloured juices. Fill the bowl with fruit, alternating with the occasional slice of bread. Pour over all the remaining liquid before covering with a final slice of bread.

Place a saucer over the pudding, add a weight and chill for about a day.

Meanwhile make a dark rich sauce from 350 g/12 oz of raspberries, 1 tablespoon of icing sugar and some lemon juice. Purée the raspberries and strain the purée, then whisk it until it is velvet-smooth.

Unmould the pudding on a white plate and pour the sauce over it, until it is deeply stained a beautiful burgundy colour.

Take the most graceful of all the berries, a sprig of white currants and a few sweet, wild strawberries and use them to decorate the pudding with a sprig of mint and a little crème chantilly, prepared as in the recipe for Strawberry swan lake (page 149).

page 100

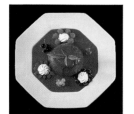

ENOUGH FOR FOUR

with oranges

Make a sugar syrup in the usual way using 50 g/2 oz sugar and 100 ml/4 fluid oz of water, and boil it for 1 minute. Remove it from the heat and add the grated rind of one lime, then allow to infuse. When the syrup is cold, squeeze in enough lime juice to suit your taste and stir the syrup well.

Cut two sweet oranges into neat segments and quarter four strawberries. Arrange the fruit on a plate, pour the lime syrup round and place a ball of freshly churned vanilla ice-cream in the centre.

ENOUGH FOR ONE

page 101

To make the sorbet, take 500 g/1¼ lb of young rhubarb stalks. Cut them into equal pieces and cook them in a covered, shallow dish with 175 g/6 oz of sugar and 150 ml/¼ pint of water in a very low oven. When the rhubarb is soft, save some of the best pieces and a little of the syrup. Cool and liquidise the remainder with all the juices and strain.

Add a few spoons of water, if necessary, to thin the purée and mix well. Now, whisk an egg white to a snow and fold it into the purée. Transfer to a sorbetière, or ice cream maker, and freeze until creamy in consistency.

The little almond biscuits are made from the same batter as the Almond tuile biscuits (page 151). You will need about a dozen. This time, make the batter without the flaked almonds and smooth it into four flower-shapes on the prepared trays. To do this, cut out cardboard stencils and mark the flower shapes on the buttered and floured trays first. Bake the biscuits until golden. When the flower biscuits can be lifted from the trays, press them gently into four small bowls to curve the petals upwards.

Set the biscuit flowers out on four plain white plates. Use a hot teaspoon to make little coquille shapes of the sorbet. Place them in the flowers, pour a little of the syrup around and decorate with the reserved rhubarb and sprigs of apple mint or lemon balm.

ENOUGH FOR FOUR

page 101

Soak 4 tablespoons of oats in 5 tablespoons of warmed skimmed milk until thick and creamy, then stir in 150 g/5 oz of natural yoghurt, 4 tablespoons of roasted chopped hazelnuts, about 3 tablespoons of clear lime-flower honey and 2 tablespoons of lemon juice.

Grate 2 crisp apples, and mix these gently into the oats, together with 450 g/1 lb of sweet summer berries – strawberries, wild strawberries, blueberries and raspberries.

Spoon the colourful and cherishing mixture into four glasses and decorate with some finely sliced apple, a sprig of mint, and a fine dusting of icing sugar.

ENOUGH FOR FOUR

page 102

I like to use a fully ripe ogen melon but other types of melon may be used, depending on the season.

Prepare an ogen melon weighing about 450 g/ 1 lb, then liquidise it with 400 g/14 oz of caster sugar and the juice of a lemon. Place the purée in a sorbetière or ice cream maker to freeze until firm.

Make a very light lime sorbet from three West Indian limes. Add half their zest to 600 ml/1 pint of water and 100 g/4 oz of sugar. Dissolve the sugar over low heat before bringing the syrup to the boil. Once bubbling, remove from the heat and allow to cool.

Add the strained juice of the fruit and churn the syrup until it has a very soft, icy consistency. Whisk an egg white to a soft peak, and add it to the lime sorbet in the sorbetière.

When the sorbets are churned to a velvety smoothness, pipe them close together in four glasses and decorate with four perfect sprigs of freshly picked mint.

ENOUGH FOR FOUR

page 103

M elt 350 g/12 oz of fine, bitter chocolate over hot water, then whisk in four egg yolks and 200 ml/7 fluid oz water. Soften $1\frac{1}{2}$ leaves of gelatine in cold water, then drain them and add them to the chocolate mixture. Leave the mixture on the water bath over low heat until the gelatine has dissolved and continue to whisk, off the heat, until almost cool. Fold in 200 ml/7 fluid oz of softly whipped cream.

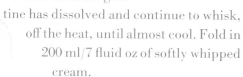

Whisk eight egg whites to a stiff, satiny sheen with 50 g/ 2 oz of sugar and fold them into the mousse. Smooth it into a glass dish and chill to set.

Make the white chocolate mousse in the same way, using half quantities and 1 leaf of gelatine.

When lightly set, use hot spoons to scoop coquilles of mousse.

Serve with a dark sauce made from 200 ml/7 fluid oz of boiling water, in which 25 g/1 oz of cocoa powder is dissolved. Over hot water, add 200 g/7 oz of bitter chocolate, chopped, and a scant 25 g/1 oz vanilla sugar.

Make another lighter sauce, using half the quantities, with milk chocolate. Finish by stirring in some double cream.

For the third sauce use half the quantities and fine, white chocolate. Replace the water and cocoa with creamy milk and finish by stirring in some double cream.

Complete the dessert by decorating it with shavings of milk chocolate, which provide a delightful, contrasting brittleness to this otherwise smooth and sensual dessert.

ENOUGH FOR EIGHT

page 104

Whole pears are carefully peeled and cored to accentuate their rounded curves, allowing one per person. Then they are poached in a sugar syrup with lemon juice and a vanilla pod, and left to cool in the poaching liquor.

Meanwhile biscuit orchids are made from the almond batter which is used to make Almond tuile biscuits (page 151). Before baking the biscuits, two fine lines of chocolate are piped around the petals. When golden brown, the biscuits are drawn from the oven and placed inside bowls to cool and become crisp.

The saffron ice cream within the orchid biscuits is made from seven egg yolks, 150 g/5 oz of sugar, 450 ml/$\frac{3}{4}$ pint of milk in the same way as the vanilla sauce which is served with the Parfait of raspberries and vanilla (page 152). A strained infusion of a few strands of saffron in a scant tablespoon of water is enough to flavour and colour the ice cream. Stir the saffron vanilla sauce over ice to chill it, then strain it and add 250 ml/8 fluid oz of double cream. Churn the ice cream in a sorbetière or ice cream maker until creamy.

Each poached pear is enrobed in a smooth, set vanilla sauce (as for the Parfait of raspberries and vanilla). Pipe a scarlet spiral of raspberry purée around the coated pears, then draw the point of a cocktail stick upwards through the sauce and the thread of purée. Then set each pear on a plate.

Near the pears, place a golden orb of saffron ice cream in each of the orchid biscuits and decorate with sprigs of mint. Serve a cut strawberry with each dessert.

page 105

ENOUGH FOR SIX

To make the vanilla sauce you will need five egg yolks, 50 g/2 oz of vanilla sugar, a vanilla pod and 350 ml/12 fluid oz half and half, milk and double cream.

Whisk the yolks with the sugar until pale and thick. Cut the vanilla pod open and scrape it out into the milk, then scald it with the milk and cream. Pour the cream and milk over the yolks, stirring all the time, then return the sauce to the pan and cook it very gently to thicken it, stirring.

Strain the sauce into a clean bowl and stir it as it cools. The sauce should be silky smooth with a lingering scent and flavour of vanilla.

Make the meringue from three egg whites: whisk them until they are stiff but not dry. Weigh 160 g/5$\frac{1}{4}$ oz of vanilla sugar and whisk 1 tablespoon of it into the egg white foam. Continue to whisk, pouring in the sugar in a gradual, steady stream until satiny and stiff.

Have ready greased baking sheets. Pipe eight wings with a star tube, in the shape of a shell. Use a smaller tube to pipe the graceful necks. Dry out the meringues in a low oven at 110°C/225°F/Gas $\frac{1}{4}$ for four to six hours, until crisp but not coloured.

To make a crème chantilly, whisk 150 ml/$\frac{1}{4}$ pint of double cream with 1 teaspoon of icing sugar and a few drops of pure vanilla essence. Melt 50 g/2 oz of fine, bitter chocolate over hot water and add 1 tablespoon of groundnut oil.

Pour the vanilla sauce into four black plates, and pipe five lines of chocolate near the side of the plate. Marble the chocolate into the sauce using a cocktail stick. Use a little chocolate sauce to tip the 'beak ends' of the swans' heads and to mark eyes. Pipe crème chantilly to sandwich the wings and necks in place. Slice six strawberries and arrange them between the wings.

Set the swans to glide on the sauce in pairs.

page 106

ENOUGH FOR FOUR SWANS

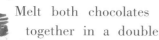

*F*irst line four moulds with a luscious chocolate cream. Use 100 g/4 oz of Swiss milk chocolate and 50 g/2 oz of Swiss bitter chocolate both finely grated. Soften 1½ leaves of gelatine in cold water. Melt both chocolates together in a double boiler, stirring. Off the heat, whisk in 90 ml/3½ fluid oz boiling double cream with 2 teaspoons of Grand Marnier.

The drained gelatine is dissolved in this dark, shining chocolate sauce. Pour this around the inside of the moulds, reserving a little. Keep the reserved sauce warm to prevent it from setting.

To make the orange mousse, blend three egg yolks with 50 g/2 oz of vanilla sugar. Scald 250 ml/8 fluid oz of milk with a vanilla pod before mixing it with the yolks; then heat the sauce very gently, stirring in the grated rind of 2 oranges, until it coats a spoon. Add 3 tablespoons of Grand Marnier and strain the sauce.

Soften 3½ leaves of gelatine in cold water. Then drain and dissolve them in the warm orange cream. Stir the mixture over a bowl of crushed ice until it begins to lightly set at the edges. Quickly fold in 250 ml/8 fluid oz of whipped cream and pour the orange cream into the centre of the chocolate-lined moulds.

When completely set, smooth the reserved chocolate over the top to seal the orange mousse and its perfume within.

Unmould the mousses and serve with a vanilla cream sauce similar to the one served with the Parfait of raspberries and vanilla (page 152). Marble some bitter chocolate, melted with a little oil to make it flow, into the vanilla cream sauce. Garnish each mousse with two segments of sweet orange, a sprig of mint, and the lightest dusting of icing sugar.

ENOUGH FOR FOUR

*W*hisk six egg whites with 200 g/7 oz of vanilla sugar, adding the sugar in a continual stream after the eggs have been whipped until stiff but not dry.

Using a wide star nozzle, pipe rosettes of the meringue on to wetted baking parchment paper. Using the tip of a palette knife, slip a few of the rosettes off the paper into 600 ml/1 pint of simmering milk in a shallow pan. Keep the pan of milk just below boiling point as you gently poach the rosettes for 3 to 4 minutes on each side.

Use a skimmer, or large, flat, slotted spoon, to lift out the rosettes and drain them on a cloth.

Make a vanilla sauce similar to the one served with the Parfait of raspberries and vanilla (page 152), using egg yolks, vanilla sugar, milk and cream. Infuse the milk with a vanilla pod, from which all the seeds are scooped into the sauce. Strain the sauce to make it very smooth and shiny.

To make the caramel cobwebs you need to boil 75 g/3 oz of sugar with about 150 ml/¼ pint of water, until the syrup has bubbled to a dark, transparent tea colour; do this in a small pan. Plunge the base of the pan into cold water to stop the caramel from darkening further. Either pipe the caramel into a delicate web when cool enough, or draw it into fine patterns on to parchment paper brushed with oil using the tines of a fork.

Carefully place the snow eggs on the sauce, set the caramel on top and scatter over a few freshly toasted flaked almonds.

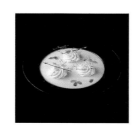

ENOUGH FOR SIX

FRUIT COOLER

You will need 75 g/3 oz each of strawberries, raspberries and blackberries; 75 g/3 oz of ripe golden mango flesh, and the same of peeled kiwi fruit. Reserve the best strawberries to decorate the glasses. Purée each fruit separately adding some lemon juice and about a tablespoon of icing sugar to make the purées smooth and thick enough to cling to the back of a spoon. The flavours should be clear and fresh.

Pass each purée through a sieve, then fill four tall cocktail glasses, beginning with blackberry and mango, then adding raspberry, kiwi and strawberry. Decorate with the reserved strawberries.

ENOUGH FOR FOUR

CRUSHED RAINBOW ICE

Make a sugar syrup of 300 ml/½ pint of water and 50 g/2 oz of sugar, boiling it for 3 minutes with a small bunch of lemon balm leaves and the juice of a small orange and lime. Strain the sauce into four flat rectangular containers and cool.

Add some burgundy to one container, some lime juice to another and a few spoonfuls of mango and raspberry purée to the remaining two portions. Place in the freezer. When they start to freeze around the edges of the containers, stir each portion of syrup with a spoon. Repeat every 20 minutes or so, until the contents of each container looks like a snowy mass of colourful, crushed ice.

Transfer the crushed ice from the containers to two beautiful crystal goblets and serve it as a refresher, instead of a sorbet – it is less sweet, and usually more natural in flavour.

ENOUGH FOR TWO

page 108

page 109

PARFAIT OF GRAND MARNIER

with passion fruit sauce

For this lovely summer parfait, whisk five egg whites with 1 tablespoon of caster sugar until foamy, then gradually add 75 g/3 oz of vanilla sugar, continuing to whisk, and the whites will mount to satiny snow.

Whisk almost 600 ml/1 pint of chilled whipping cream until it can be raised to a peak and, separately, whisk 2 small egg yolks with 1 tablespoon each of vanilla sugar and Grand Marnier. Gently fold the Grand Marnier mixture into the whipped cream, then fold in the egg whites and mix until all three foams are softly and evenly blended. Smooth the parfait mixture into a mould and freeze until set.

Make six frilled biscuit cups, following the Almond tuile biscuit recipe (right).

The clear, golden passion fruit sauce is made by scooping the flesh of six small ripe passion fruit into a small bowl. The fruit shells, 100 g/4 oz of sugar and 300 ml/½ pint of water are simmered together for 20 minutes before the fruit is added and simmered for a further 3 minutes. Add a little orange juice to taste: the juice of about a quarter of an orange is all that is required.

Mix a very small amount of arrowroot with 1 tablespoon of cold water, and simmer this with the rest of the sauce for a minute. Strain the clear and rosy sauce through a fine sieve, then replace a few seeds to give character.

To serve the parfait, unmould it and slice it with a hot knife. Divide the slices between six plates and decorate with the almond cups filled with passion fruit: you will need about six of the little dark fruit, or three of the much larger variety called grenadillas.

Pour the passion fruit sauce around and decorate with raspberry hearts. These are made by dropping dots of raspberry sauce from a teaspoon on to the golden sauce and drawing the tip of a cocktail stick through the centre.

page 110

ENOUGH FOR SIX

ALMOND TUILE BISCUITS

Prepare almond tuile biscuits to accompany the dessert course. Bring an egg white to room temperature. Mix 50 g/2 oz of unsalted butter, 60 g/2¼ oz of caster sugar, a pinch of salt and a few drops of pure vanilla essence together, then add the egg white and the flour to make a smooth batter. Mix in 25 g/1 oz flaked almonds and rest the batter in a cool place for 30 minutes.

To bake the biscuits, drop 6 tablespoons of the batter, at a distance from each other, on two or more lavishly buttered baking sheets, which have been also dusted with flour. With wetted fingertips, spread the batter in wide and wild circles, so only the finest, barest film remains.

Bake the biscuits in a preheated oven at 180°C/350°F/Gas 4 for about 8 minutes, until golden. Make six little frilled biscuit cups by pressing the biscuits into demi-tasse cups or small deep patty tins immediately they can be removed from the baking sheets.

ENOUGH FOR SIX

*T*ake two bananas, peel them and cut them in half.

Make a golden sauce from the juice of three passion fruit, separated from their seeds by liquidising briefly and straining them. Mix with 1 tablespoon of sugar syrup and add a few of the passion fruit seeds.

Place the bananas and sauce in two neat and gleaming pouches made carefully from silver foil. Add a few slices of orange and lemon, two halved strawberries and half of a vanilla pod to each package. Place in a hot oven at 200°C/400°F/Gas 6 for 10 to 12 minutes.

When bubbling hot, transfer the packages to pretty plates and open the foil pouches in front of your guests.

Now add the finishing touches: place a sprig of mint inside each pouch and dust with icing sugar.

ENOUGH FOR TWO

page 111

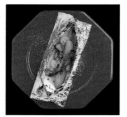

*W*hen you make the parfait you will need an oblong mould, which can be sealed and placed in the freezer. Whisk five egg yolks with 175 g/6 oz sugar in a double boiler or basin over hot water until thick and creamy. Take the basin off the simmering water and continue to whisk until cool. Whip 200 ml/7 fluid oz of double cream and fold it into the mixture. Whisk three egg whites to a snow and fold this carefully and gently into the eggs and sugar with 1 teaspoon of pure vanilla essence.

Pour the mixture into the mould and place in the freezer at an angle, so that the vanilla parfait settles into the corner along one side of the mould. Freeze until firm.

Purée 225 g/8 oz fresh, ripe raspberries in perfect condition and strain. Whisk with enough lemon juice and a little icing sugar to make a deeply coloured, excellently flavoured purée.

Make a second parfait in the same way, adding 150 ml/¼ pint of raspberry purée to the basic mixture. Pour this over the frozen vanilla parfait, and return to the freezer until firm.

Make a vanilla cream sauce (below) to serve with the parfait. The parfait will serve about ten to twelve, so you will need a small basket of fresh raspberries and a bunch of young mint. Place a few raspberries on each plate, add a sprig of mint and dust with icing sugar. Add the vanilla cream sauce to the plates. Pour raspberry purée down the outside edge of the vanilla cream sauce; marble the sauces outwards. Lay parfait slices gently on the sauce.

VANILLA CREAM SAUCE

Make a vanilla cream sauce with five egg yolks and 125 g/4½ oz of vanilla sugar whisked to a ribbon. Add 300 ml/½ pint of scalded milk, 150 ml/¼ pint of single cream and about 1 teaspoon of pure vanilla essence. As this cools, stir in 150 ml/¼ pint of double cream.

ENOUGH FOR TEN TO TWELVE

page 113

CHOCOLATE MOUSSE
with white and dark chocolate sauces

Soften 1 leaf of gelatine in cold water. Oil eight moulds. Cut 200 g/7 oz of finest Swiss chocolate into pieces and melt it over hot water with 2 tablespoons each of strong black coffee and Cognac, and the drained gelatine. Beat five egg yolks with 40 g/1½ oz of caster sugar, until the sugar has dissolved.

Stir the yolk mixture into the chocolate, taking care to ensure that the chocolate does not cool, or it will set before all the ingredients are added. Whisk five egg whites to a snow with 50 g/2 oz of caster sugar. Fold in 150 ml/¼ pint of whipped double cream followed quickly by the whisked whites. Smooth the mousse lightly into the prepared moulds. Cover the moulds and chill.

To make the chocolate sauce, cut up 225/8 oz of the finest, dark chocolate and melt it in the top of a double boiler. Stir in 75 ml/3 fluid oz of syrup made with equal quantities of sugar and water. Gradually blend the chocolate mixture into about 150 ml/¼ pint of cream.

Finely chop 50 g/2 oz each of milk chocolate and white chocolate and melt them separately over hot water. Stir 1 tablespoon of ground nut oil into each until smooth and glossy.

Pour some of the dark chocolate sauce on to a plate, tapping the plate on the surface to spread it into a dark and shining circle. Unmould one mousse and place it in the middle. Pipe a circle of the white chocolate around the edge, then one of the milk chocolate inside that. Spin a little dark chocolate sauce over the mousse. Marble the white and milk sauces. Decorate with curls of white chocolate. Serve the remaining mousses in the same way.

page 114

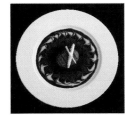

ENOUGH FOR EIGHT

FIG SORBET
with fresh figs and oranges

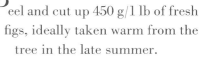

Peel and cut up 450 g/1 lb of fresh figs, ideally taken warm from the tree in the late summer.

Each fig should be in perfect condition – soft, ripe and deeply coloured within. Cook them with 300 ml/½ pint of light sugar syrup, the juice of a lemon and a cinnamon stick for 2 to 3 minutes. Remove the cinnamon stick and purée the fruit and the syrup. Allow the purée to cool, then freeze it in a sorbetière, or ice cream maker, until it has a smooth, creamy consistency.

Make the sauce with the juice of ten oranges, strained into a pan and sweetened with sugar to taste. Blend ¼ teaspoon of cornflour with a little orange juice, then add it to the pan and bring the sauce to the boil, stirring occasionally. Reduce the sauce slightly, then leave it to cool, stirring occasionally.

Cut six figs into quarters and cut away the pith and peel from some oranges. Then cut out beautiful orange segments.

Pour a little of the sauce on to each plate. Arrange orange segments in the sauce and the figs around the sauce. Place a swirl of sorbet in the centre. Decorate with a few very finely cut pistachios.

ENOUGH FOR SIX

page 115

*T*ake one pear, in perfect condition. Peel, core and halve it, then cut it across into slices.

Arrange the slices on a buttered baking sheet and sprinkle with icing sugar. Place under a very hot preheated grill until the edges brown.

The slices of each pear half are placed between the finest squares of almond batter pastry and dusted with icing sugar, sprinkled through a stencil.

While still warm it is arranged on this marvellous, coloured plate, so the pastry may be eaten at its most fragile, while the pear is moist and juicy.

ENOUGH FOR TWO

page 116

*T*ake 225 g/8 oz of kiwi fruit, peel the fruit and remove their white cores. Liquidise the prepared fruit briefly to free the pips. The black pips should not be broken.

Now cook 250 g/9 oz of peeled and cored apples and 200 g/7 oz of blackcurrants separately in the minimum of water with a little lemon juice and sugar until soft. When cool, purée and sieve both types of fruit separately.

Purée separately 200 g/7 oz of fine raspberries, 200 g/7 oz of strawberries, and 400 g/14 oz of mango flesh taken from its peel. Strain each purée through a fine sieve, again keeping them separate. Whisk a little icing sugar and lemon juice into each purée to enhance colour and flavour.

When all the purées are made, compare them and thin them down using mineral water, if necessary, so that they are all the same consistency. The apple purée should be thinned with apple juice. The purées should be thick enough to stand proud in a pool on the plate. Scoop or pour the purées on to four plates in the same pattern for each plate. The apple purée should form the centre.

To marble the purées, you will need to tap the plate firmly on a table or surface, holding it on opposite sides, so that the edges of the purées blend together.

Draw the end of a spoon through the purées to marble your own design. Drop a little cream into the centre of the apple purée and draw it into a delicate wisp using a cocktail stick. Add a tiny portion of raspberry purée on the cream and draw a clean cocktail stick through it to accentuate the wisp of cream.

Decorate each plate with three perfect raspberries, a fine sprig of mint and the lightest dusting of icing sugar.

ENOUGH FOR FOUR

page 117

Variety and creativity

In my portfolio of culinary art and the recipes, I have tried to pick out some of my favourite dishes but the restrictions of space will not allow me to present as many as I would like. To highlight the many ways in which I like to create with food, a montage of photographs is presented on pages 40 and 41; here I would like to discuss its content.

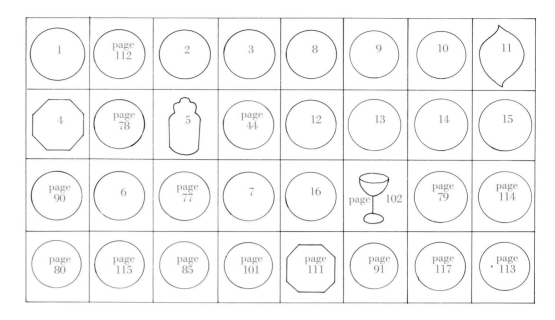

Ravioli filled with cottage cheese and served with three sauces

A silky-smooth ravioli dough is made from 400 g/14 oz of strong flour with 7 g/¼ oz of salt, 3 tablespoons of groundnut oil, two eggs and 3 to 4 tablespoons of water.

The filling is based on 450 g/1 lb of cottage cheese with salt, freshly milled pepper and 2 tablespoons of chopped chives, and, if you wish, 25 g/1 oz each of carrots cut into fine dice and sliced truffles. This gives both colour, texture and flavour to the filling.

A white wine sauce forms the base for two of the sauces. One portion is flavoured with infused saffron; the second has a few dice of carrots, celery and finely cut chives added to it. The third sauce is a purée of ripe tomatoes seasoned and sharpened with lemon juice.

The ravioli are cooked until al dente in a large amount of salted water, for 4 to 5 minutes. They are drained and served with the saffron sauce, the white wine and vegetable sauce and the tomato sauce, then garnished with a few cut chives.

Creamed kipper

Kipper is under-estimated and seldom used to its full potential. For the creamed kipper, the fish is soaked in milk, then puréed and sieved. This is combined with cream and made into a mousseline by whisking over ice. The mousseline is poached in a foil-lined mould. By arranging one whole fillet in a tender coat of blanched spinach in the centre of the mousseline, one is given an opportunity to appreciate the satin translucency of the flesh. The creamed kipper mould is cooled and sliced, then the slices are laid on a golden mirror of fish jelly. The little buds of tomato roses, chives and chervil leaves are added as a garnish.

A lobster consommé with trompettes de morte

A richly refined creation based on the finest of lobster consommés. Médaillons of lobster tail are served in the shimmering liquid with lobster shapes cut from carrot and celeriac. Each plate is garnished with lobster coral and perfumed by coriander leaves.

1 Ravioli filled with cottage cheese and served with three sauces
2 Creamed kipper
3 A lobster consommé with trompettes de morte
4 John Dory poached with two pepper sauces
5 Marinated goat's cheese
6 Paupiettes of sole with three-coloured peppers
7 Summer berry basket
8 Mango, lime and raspberry mousses on a mango purée
9 Grilled duck sausages on a bed of lentils
10 Grilled sea bass with tomato and yellow pepper sauces
11 Goujons of sole with twin sauces
12 A symphony of sorbets and ices
13 Wing of skate with roasted butter and baby vegetables
14 Gull's egg on spinach sauce
15 Blue fish with cabbage and bacon in butter sauce
16 Suprême de volaille jardinière

John Dory poached with two pepper sauces

Steamed fillets of John Dory are beautifully complemented by sauces of red and yellow sweet peppers. The seasoned fish fillets are steamed for 3 to 4 minutes. The sauces of yellow and red pepper are flavoured with onion, garlic, lemon thyme and basil, all cooked in fish stock, then puréed. The steamed fish is served on the sauces and a sprig of basil is the only garnish.

Marinated goat's cheese

A marinade of virgin olive oil and fresh Provençal herbs is ideal for the goat's cheese made in the mountains and ripened until firm.

When you serve the cheese, with a crusty *pain de campagne*, take care to spoon a little of the richly flavoured marinade on to the plate.

Paupiettes of sole with three-coloured peppers

Two skinned quarter fillets of sole are seasoned and rolled around six batonnets of red, green and yellow pepper, then secured with a cocktail stick. The paupiettes are poached in fish stock for 4 to 5 minutes, then served with a carefully seasoned sauce of reduced wine and Noilly Prat, with fish stock and cream. A garnish of finely cut chives completes the dish.

Summer berry basket

This is one of the loveliest ways to serve the harvest of summer berries when they are in the peak of condition at the height of their short season. The fragile crust of an almond tuile biscuit is the perfect contrast to their sweet juiciness. The biscuit cup is prepared following the recipe on page 151.

Mango, lime and raspberry mousses on a mango purée

Three fresh fruit mousses, as light as foam, are served on a bright mango sauce, decorated with a raspberry coulis, to give a peacock's feather pattern.

Take 200 g/7 oz of raspberries and 350 g/12 oz of ripe mango weighed after they have been puréed and strained. Grate the rind and squeeze the juice from three limes.

The three mousses are made in the same way: for each fruit, separate two eggs and whisk the yolks with 25 g/1 oz of caster sugar in a bowl over steaming water, until pale and thick. Now, in each of three separate basins (one for each fruit), dissolve 2 leaves of gelatine, previously softened, in 2 tablespoons of warm water. Stir a portion of gelatine into each fruit purée adding the lime juice with the grated rind. Add the yolk mixture and a little lemon juice to taste.

Stir 50 g/2 oz of fromage frais or whipped cream into each of the mousses. When the mousses are half set, fold in the egg whites, whisked to a snow, and chill each mousse to set in a shallow glass dish.

A sauce of golden mango purée, simmered with a few spoons of water and a little lemon juice, and sweetened with a little icing sugar, is served with carefully arranged quenelles of each mousse. A teaspoon of uncooked raspberry purée and a dot of reduced raspberry purée are added and drawn with a cocktail stick into an imaginative decoration.

Grilled duck sausages on a bed of lentils

These crisp, richly browned sausages enclose a filling that is balanced in both texture and flavour. Dark fillets of duck breast are finely chopped to retain some texture. The seasoning is added with great care to accentuate, rather than disguise, the fullness of the meat.

Here the grilled sausage is served on a carefully prepared bed of nutty green lentils.

Grilled sea bass with tomato and yellow pepper sauce

A fine-flavoured fish in a dramatic presentation with two sauces of tomato and sweet yellow pepper. The tomato sauce is based on 450 g/1 lb of the most flavoursome, ripe tomatoes, simmered with a little shallot and red pepper, bay leaf, thyme and parsley. The yellow pepper sauce is a simple purée of pepper simmered in fish stock. The fish is grilled for about 3 minutes on each side before it is served.

Goujons of sole with twin sauces

*T*he two vibrantly coloured sauces contrast with the pure, white flesh of the poached sole. The tomato sauce is a purée of simmered tomatoes, seasoned and sharpened with lemon juice, then strained.

The yellow sauce is a reduction of white wine and fish stock, thickened with a little double cream and flavoured with steeped saffron. The vivid sauce is strained and carefully seasoned before taking its place alongside the tomato sauce.

Slender strips of skinned and filleted sole, lightly seasoned and gently poached in a richly flavoured fish stock, are arranged on the sauces and two delicate leaves of chervil are the only garnish.

A symphony of sorbets and ices

A favourite dessert from *Cuisine Naturelle*, here I combine four sorbets and iced specialities with freshly prepared exotic fruits.

The pale yellow sorbet is a refreshing combination of lime juice and infused saffron – perfect for serving between the fish and meat courses of a meal or an interesting accompaniment to the other fruit-flavoured ices that are illustrated.

Wing of skate with roasted butter and baby vegetables

*A*n opaquely fresh wing of skate is poached in fish stock, then served with jewel-like vegetables that are blanched and refreshed before they are tossed in hot golden butter.

Colour comes from a leaf of a young Savoy cabbage, two turnips, some mange tout and a peeled tomato. Button onions, carrots and baby corn are tossed in butter before all the remaining vegetables are added.

The skate is dressed with a spoonful of butter scented with a teaspoon of sliced truffle.

Gull's egg on spinach sauce

I like to serve gull's eggs as simply as possible. Here, the egg is served with a sauce of spinach puréed with cream and a sprinkling of sea salt on a lustrous black plate. Now you can see the intense yellow of the yolk, and the graceful sheen on the curves of the shell.

Bluefish with cabbage and bacon in butter sauce

I am always fascinated and excited by the many species of fish that are sold at the market. This fine specimen, with its blue-grey sheen, comes from the deep waters of the Atlantic and Mediterranean. It has a richly flavoured, firm flesh that is matched by the accompanying shredded smoked bacon and lightly cooked cabbage.

Suprême de volaille au jardinière

*E*very time I make this I am delighted afresh by the colours, flavours and textures of the vegetables, and their contrast to the smooth flesh of the chicken breast. A choice of carrots, courgettes, radishes, yellow pepper, raw beetroot and carrots, cut into julienne strips are served with chicken breasts, poached in chicken stock.

The reduced stock is flavoured with Dijon mustard and tarragon or sherry vinegar. The vegetables are tossed separately in the sauce with salt and freshly milled pepper to taste.

Each chicken breast is set on its plate and the vegetables are arranged around. Then some nicely cut chives are scattered over the chicken.

Index

Acknowledgements

Editor: Bridget Jones
Designer: Maggie Aldred
Photography: Tom Belshaw
Illustrations: Victoria Granville, Nicola Gregory
Typeset by Servis Filmsetting Limited, Manchester
Printed and bound in Italy by OFSA SPA, Milan

The contents of this publication are believed correct at the time of printing. Nevertheless, the Publishers cannot accept responsibility for errors or omissions, nor for changes in details given.

Published by Waymark Publications, an imprint of The Automobile Association, in conjunction with InFo Publishing Ltd, a member of the Spero Communications Group of Companies
Text and photographs © Anton Mosimann

A CIP catalogue record for this book is available from the British Library.
Produced and distributed in the United Kingdom by the Publishing Division of the Automobile Association, Fanum House, Basingstoke, Hampshire, RG21 2EA.
ISBN 0 86145 879 6